Grace on a Rambling Road

Devotions for RV Travelers

Congratulations, Best
Wishes for a life time of
adventures!

The Lord himself will go
before you. He will be with you;
He will not leave you or forget you.
Don't be afraid and don't worry.

Nancy Bell Kimsey

Deuteronomy
31:8

Much Love,

Published by Pine Warbler Publications
North Carolina, United States of America

GRACE ON A RAMBLING ROAD: DEVOTIONS
FOR RV TRAVELERS

First Printing, 2021

Cover Design by Savannah Battle and Nathan Stikeleather

ISBN #9781736773109 (eBook)
ISBN #9781736773116 (Paperback)

To Ray, my wonderful husband and partner on the road of life.

Your Treasure

For where your treasure is, there your heart will be also. Luke 12:34

Several months elapsed between the period when we began to seriously consider ordering a custom travel trailer and the day when we drove away from the factory as proud owners. During those months we spent untold hours researching options, checking our finances, planning our first camping trip, and ordering scores of tools and accessories. I began to feel as though I should bake some cookies for our package delivery driver! As the piles of items in our garage and on the dining room table grew higher, so did our excitement level.

Whether our "treasure" is invested in purchasing an RV, increasing expertise in a hobby, or supporting our children's sports teams, it's not only money that is being spent. We are also consuming time, using mental energy, and creating new associations and friendships. All of these combine to grab hold of our hearts, and we begin to think and talk of little else. There is nothing wrong with having treasure in our lives, but we should not allow any possession or activity to become more important to us than our relationship with God.

What are some practical ways that we can keep God in the forefront of our affections? We can ask God to help us to truthfully evaluate the current priorities of our heart's devotion. We can keep track of the amount of time that we spend on different activities (including preparation, participation, and social media related to that activity.) We can set aside time, money, and mental energy so that our lives are not too full to respond to God's leading. Finally, we can ask someone that we trust to honestly speak to us if we become fixated on any activity or possession.

Prayer for Today:

Dear God, my mind, heart, time, and energy
are often absorbed with the treasures that you
have graciously given to me. Please help me
to notice when I think and behave as if they are
more important than You. May I joyously put
you first today. Amen.

Rubbernecking

We hear that some among you are idle and disruptive. They are not busy; they are busybodies. 2 Thessalonians 3:11

Brake lights glowed ahead of us in a crimson column. Ugh, a wreck! After many minutes of inching forward, we finally reached the scene of the accident. The cars involved in the wreck had already been moved off the road, but passers-by continued to creep on, "rubbernecking" to look for any gory details. Onlooker delay was extending the life of the traffic jam. Even while I grumbled at the snail's pace of the observers, it was hard not to succumb to the temptation to stare at the scene myself.

There is an old saying, "Curiosity killed the cat." I suppose the cat died from poking his nose into a dangerous situation. Or, thinking outside the box, the cat could have died from being so curious about something that he forgot to eat. Or perhaps the cat was a gossip-loving busybody whose fellow cats got so annoyed that they decided to do away with him!

The Bible condemns busybodies and links their actions to idleness and disruption. People with nothing better to do are easily drawn in to conversations with other meddlers. Passing on information in an outwardly pious show of concern can

3

become an excuse for engaging in gossip. Instead, we need to be occupied with projects, prayers, or acts of service which honor God. Some synonyms for the word *disrupt* are *wreck, upset,* and *disturb.* Busybodies disrupt relationships and create hard feelings and disorder. Proverbs 16:28 warns, *A perverse person stirs up conflict, and a gossip separates close friends.*

When I drive by a roadside accident, I can try to move past smoothly and pray for those involved. When I am tempted to pass on a juicy piece of gossip as a "prayer request", I can ask God to grant me the self-discipline to pray on my own and keep the information private.

Prayer for Today:

May the words of my mouth and the
meditations of my heart be acceptable in thy
sight, dear God. Help me to critically examine
my speech and my motives. Rescue me from
idle curiosity, and may I be a peacemaker in
this world. Amen.

Cinnamon Roll Fail

Then Peter remembered the word Jesus had spoken: "Before the rooster crows, you will disown me three times." And he went outside and wept bitterly. Matthew 26:75

In an attempt to broaden my range of fire pit cooking options beyond hot dogs on a roasting stick, I researched all sorts of campfire cuisine. Most of the recipes involved sealing ingredients in foil packets or using skewers. I was filled with pride when I successfully cooked a packet of salmon with herbs, cherry tomatoes, and frozen corn kernels while boondocking. The *pièce de résistance* for the meal was going to be a new dessert: cinnamon rolls on a stick.

The idea of the recipe was to wrap the cinnamon roll dough around a skewer, hold it over the flames, and finally dip the fire-baked twists in frosting. The pictured creations were golden brown and fluffy, but the reality was quite the opposite. As we cooked the treats, they began to unravel and droop off the skewers like a Salvador Dali painting. The dough burned in some areas and was a goopy mess in others. Epic fail! Less than an hour had passed between confidence and catastrophe.

After the Last Supper, Peter proudly promised Jesus that he would remain faithful at all costs, but Christ foreknew that

5

Peter would soon deny Him three times. This same Peter had already been declared by Christ to be the rock on which the church would be built. When Peter realized what he had done, he wept bitterly over his actions. Yet he was later able to move forward because of the grace of Christ. Jesus forgave Peter for his prideful failures and equipped him for future service.

Prayer for Today:

Dear Lord, you know the end from the beginning. You know that I have often failed you. This day, may I rest in the knowledge that you forgive sins when your children seek repentance. You have the power to transform my life. Please use me for your glory, today and always. Amen.

Be the Thermostat

He got up, rebuked the wind and said to the waves, "Quiet! Be still!"
Then the wind died down and it was completely calm. Mark 4:39

Do you and your traveling companion disagree about an optimum temperature for the interior of your RV? Perhaps you engage in a clandestine "war of the thermostat", adjusting the desired temperature bit by bit and hoping that the other person doesn't notice.

You may have heard this phrase in a business seminar or parenting workshop: "Be the thermostat, not the thermometer." The interpretation for someone in a business setting might be that leaders should set the course for the company, rather than constantly reacting to the actions of others. Parents could be admonished to set a level of emotional stability that doesn't break down when the children demonstrate mood swings. In both situations, the goal is to not simply reflect your surroundings but to pre-set the desired result.

Jesus maintained an inner calmness in all types of circumstances: through long difficult days teaching and traveling, through fierce interrogation and torture. Sometimes Jesus became the thermostat by changing the physical environment that surrounded him. One such instance, recorded in the book of Mark, was when Christ calmed a storm at sea. *He got up, rebuked the wind and said to the waves, "Quiet! Be still!" Then the wind died down and it was completely calm.* Mark 4:39

Even when Christ did not choose to alter his situation, He was always in control as God incarnate. A very interesting scene took place in the Garden of Gethsemane when Judas, a detachment of soldiers, and some religious officials came to arrest Jesus. The book of John describes Jesus at that moment as *knowing all that was going to happen to him,* (John 18:4) so we know that Christ was divinely aware of the horrors to come. When Jesus acknowledged his identity verbally, those who had come to arrest him actually drew back and fell to the ground! At that point, Jesus could have called down legions of angels to pull him out of danger, but instead he calmly requested that the disciples be allowed to leave and submitted to his own arrest.

Although we do not have the power to completely control the situations that swirl around us, we can resolve to maintain calmness and plan a course of action that will lead to more positive results. Under the guidance of the Holy Spirit, we can be a thermostat, setting a course of peace and stability, rather than a reactionary thermometer.

Prayer for Today:

O Lord, you have the power to calm the sea of confusion in which I often find myself. You also can give me guidance as I seek to walk in peace with others and to find calmness within myself. Please help me not to react to others but to seek you in all situations. Amen.

Mama Bear

Just as a nursing mother cares for her children, so we cared for you. Because we loved you so much, we were delighted to share with you not only the gospel of God but our lives as well. 1 Thessalonians 2:7-8

The forest green bus lumbered down a narrow road as we traveled into the heart of Denali National Park in Alaska. Our National Parks Service tour guide gave a running commentary on the history of the region, the animals that we hoped to see, and our chances of actually being able to view Denali (formerly called Mount McKinley) on that day. All of the guides kept in constant communication with one another, and as the guides or their passengers saw a particular animal, the news would be passed around. Several hours into our journey, the cry went out from a passenger on our bus, "Grizzly bears on the right!" Our driver was able to pull over on the narrow shoulder, and everyone grabbed their cameras and cell phones. A mama polar bear and her two cubs were at the crest of a snow-covered hill. We watched, transfixed, as a scene unfolded that was so perfect it could have been part of a nature documentary.

The mother bear and one of the cubs slid down the hill in a flurry of flying snow, but the other cub remained at the top, perhaps too afraid or reluctant to proceed. Mama paced back and forth at the bottom for some time, but cub number two would not budge. Eventually the mother bear lumbered part way up the steep slope. We laughed, imagining that she was calling out, "I said to get down here now! Don't make me come all the way up this hill!" Finally, the reluctant cub cruised down the hill and landed with a tumble.

In Paul's letter to the Thessalonians, he compares his relationship to the believers from that city to that of a nursing mother who shares her very life with her children. Paul was not merely a preacher who breezed into town, shared the gospel, and moved on. He genuinely cared for the individuals in the churches and invested his life to encourage and strengthen them. Although he sometimes had to communicate with words of chastisement, he was willing, even delighted, to "travel up the hill" and help them make progress along the correct path.

Prayer for Today:

Dear God, all that you have created reveals
your wisdom and creativity. It is a joy to
watch mother animals as they instinctively care
for their babies. Help me to act in wisdom and
love toward those whom you have put in my
path. May I be sincerely delighted to
unselfishly share my life as I share the Gospel.
Amen.

Throw off the Weight

Therefore, since we are surrounded by such a great cloud of witnesses, let us throw off everything that hinders and the sin that so easily entangles. And let us run with perseverance the race marked out for us, fixing our eyes on Jesus, the pioneer and perfecter of faith.
Hebrews 12:1-2

Weight is an enemy of the RV traveler, and the battle with weight is constant. Too many items in the camper or the truck bed can cause us to exceed our tow capacity, setting up a dangerous situation. When we first purchased our travel trailer, we set up a spreadsheet and weighed a host of items that we planned to carry along on trips. Even the weight of small items added up quickly and could affect our gas mileage and safety. Since we weren't interested in leaving a family member behind to lighten things up, some downsizing was in order.

The Bible uses the metaphor of running a race to illustrate the Christian life. We are exhorted to throw off everything that hinders our progress on the route. Sin is described as something that entangles - a very accurate image! Try to envision a runner yanking off a heavy backpack and jumping out of a convoluted rope. Once the weights and snares have been eliminated, the runner feels exhilarated and free. In the same way, if we leave behind bad habits, poor attitudes, and other sins, we can experience joyful liberation.

The motivation for clearing our lives of hindrances and sin is to remember those who have faithfully run the race before us. The running analogy of Hebrews chapter 12 is preceded by the description of several all-stars of faith in Hebrews chapter 11, including Abel, Enoch, Noah, and Abraham. The method for running the race of faith successfully and with perseverance is *fixing our eyes on Jesus, the pioneer and perfecter of faith.* (Hebrews 12:2) Remember the examples of our faith heritage, deliberately throw off the weight of sin, and look to Jesus today.

Prayer for Today:

Dear Lord, thank you for the example of your
faithful servants throughout history. I know
that there are areas of disobedience in my life
that have entangled me for a long time.
Through faith, I pledge to push them aside to
follow you. Grant me perseverance, and may I
more purely live for you. Amen.

Star Hike

When I consider your heavens, the work of your fingers, the moon and the stars, which you have set in place, what is mankind that you are mindful of them, human beings that you care for them? Psalm 8:3-4

My childhood was filled with camping, both with my family and with the Girl Scouts. I loved that our Scout troop (whose fearless leader was my mother) went on far more camping trips per year than most others. Merit badges could be fun, but hiking and tending a fire were ten times better! When night fell and the campfire had faded to embers, we would settle in to our sleeping bags, ready to sleep...or maybe not! Giggling and yakking sounds would continue until Mom appeared at the entrance to the tent, informing us that we were all going to head out immediately on a star hike. Off we would go to the nearest open area where we could gaze up in wonder at the astounding panoply of stars. She knew that after 45 minutes or so of tromping around in the dark and learning to identify constellations, we would sleep like babies.

The awesome night sky fills us with wonder and a sense of how tiny we are in comparison to the breadth of the cosmos. Our galaxy alone, the Milky Way, is estimated to contain about 100 thousand million stars. It has been well said that one of the most understated sentences in the Bible is found in Genesis 1:16. *He also made the stars.*

When Jesus walked on Earth, he did not treat individuals as mere pawns in a giant game of celestial chess or ignore their needs. Each one had been made in the image of God: worthy of being heard, worthy of healing, persons for whom He would give his life. We are specks in the universe, but we are valuable to God.

Prayer for Today:

O awesome God, you are beyond comprehension in your majesty, power, and creativity. Thank you for the stars that point us to you. Thank you that your Word reveals how much you care fo me as an individual. May I rest in the knowledge that you know me and care for me. Amen.

Vintage Camper

"The days are coming, declares the Lord, when I will make a new covenant with the people of Israel and with the people of Judah.". . .By calling this covenant "new" he has made the first one obsolete; and what is obsolete and outdated will soon disappear. (Hebrews 8:8,13)

In recent years, there has been a resurgence in the restoration of vintage campers. If you look up the word *vintage* in a thesaurus, you will find that when used as an adjective, it has two rather different sets of synonyms. One set involves pleasant memories of the past: (*quaint, retro*). The other set is more derogatory: (*outdated, old-school*). Those who take on these renovation projects often find that a vintage camper can embody both meanings! That adorable rig can also contain obsolete appliances or an aging roof.

The writer of the Book of Hebrews describes God's former covenant with the people of Israel and Judah as *obsolete* and *outdated*. The old covenant was based on ceremonial regulations and sacrifices offered by the priests. *How much more, then, will the blood of Christ, who through the eternal Spirit offered himself unblemished to God, cleanse our consciences from acts that lead to death, so that we may serve the living God! For this reason Christ is the mediator of a new covenant, that those who are called may receive the promised eternal inheritance.* (Hebrews 9:14-15)

We can be thankful that Christ's sacrificial death on the cross provides a way for us to be made clean in God's sight. This new covenant will never become obsolete, and forgiveness is always available.

Prayer for Today:

Dear God, I thank you that you have provided a way for my sins to be forgiven and my conscience to be cleansed. Thank you for the assurance of salvation and eternal life through the new covenant.   Amen.

Too Much of a Good Thing

*If you find honey, eat just enough - too much of it, and you will vomit.
Seldom set foot in your neighbor's house - too much of you, and they
will hate you.* Proverbs 25:16-18

One summer while home from college, I made a new friend at my seasonal job. This guy owned a mandolin, and I enjoyed singing along with the old-time music that he would play. One weekend, several of us decided to attend a bluegrass festival together. We assembled a ragtag collection of tarps, tents, snacks, and of course the mandolin, and headed to Galax, Virginia. At first, it was exciting to wander around the outdoor venue, visit the various stages, listen to the bluegrass performers, and sing along with impromptu jam sessions. But about halfway through the second day, I suddenly felt as though I would lose my mind if I heard one more bluegrass song! We were also getting sunburned, sweaty, and grumpy from lack of sleep. Our group left before the end of the festival, having had our fill of bluegrass for some time to come.

There are numerous situations in life which require wisdom and self-control so that we do not become over-filled. It's obvious that too many nachos can lead to discomfort, and too many cocktails can lead to danger. But it's less obvious that too much talking can leave those around you feeling left out or annoyed. Too many visits to your neighbor's house or religious messages on social media can alienate those whom we most want to find hope in God.

My father used to say, "When you are in the hospital, you can't wait for people to come and visit you. And when they get there, you can't wait for them to leave." He also seldom stayed at anyone's home for more than three consecutive days. No danger of my dad wearing out his welcome! Perhaps he took things a bit too far, but overall he had the right idea.

Prayer for Today:

Dear Lord, I need to control my appetite and my tongue. I need to think critically about how I am viewed by others, and how my actions may make them feel. Please fill me with your wisdom and with the desire to obey when you whisper to me, "That's enough." Amen.

The Geezer Pass

Teach us to number our days, that we may gain a heart of wisdom.
Psalm 90:12

The National Park Service offers citizens who are age 62 and older a special lifetime pass that allows the bearer and three adult traveling companions to enter most national parks for free, as well as providing discounts on entry and camping fees in some other federal lands. This senior pass was once called the Golden Age Passport and used to cost only $10. In 2017, the price increased to $80, and the pass was given the rather wordy new name of America the Beautiful: The National Parks and Federal Recreational Lands Senior Pass. Maybe the federal government hoped that we wouldn't mind the price increase if the program had a more fancy-schmancy name! I suggest that a free pass be offered to anyone willing to carry a card entitled The Geezer Pass.

Kidding aside, the pass is a wonderful bargain, even if you only live a few years more after making your purchase. Any investment made as a senior is a bit of a gamble, but we all like to believe that we will live to a ripe old age. In reality, none of us is promised tomorrow. Psalm 39:5 reminds us, *You have made my days a mere handbreadth; the span of my years is as nothing before you. Everyone is but a breath, even those who seem secure.* When we recognize the brevity of life, we are much more likely to use our hours and days wisely. We will be also willing to put aside long-held grudges and seek reconciliation before the opportunity to do so escapes us. Finally, we will be controlled by the perspective that we are sojourners on Earth, living here for a brief time before relocating to our heavenly home.

Prayer for Today:

Dear Lord, I want to have a heart of wisdom, so teach me to number my days. Please show me how to use this day in a way that honors you. If I need to reconcile with someone, may I overcome my reluctance and hard feelings so that peace may be restored. Throughout every day that has been ordained for me, may I remember that heaven is my home. Amen.

A Rig by Any Other Name

*Moses said to God, "Suppose I go to the Israelites and say to them,
'The God of your fathers has sent me to you,' and they ask me, 'What
is his name?' Then what shall I tell them?'" God said to Moses, "I
AM WHO I AM. This is what you are to say to the Israelites: 'I
AM has sent me to you.'"* Exodus 3:13-14

Does your rig have a name? Many travelers enjoy
christening their RVs with names that range from quirky to
sentimental. Some names evoke wanderlust, others are
reminders of home towns or dear family members, but none are
random. In the Bible, names are important for their underlying
meaning. The angel instructed Mary to give her son the name
Jesus *because he will save his people from their sins.* (Matthew
1:21) Christ changed Simon's name to Peter (Rock) and
promised him, *on this rock I will build my church, and the
gates of Hades will not overcome it.* (Matthew 16:18)
There are many different names for God in the Scriptures.
Each one reveals something about the nature and character of
God. Meditating on the names of God is a wonderful way to
remind ourselves of His faithfulness, power, and eternality.
Enjoy pondering some of them today.

Jehovah– Jireh: the Lord will Provide (Genesis 22:14)

Alpha and Omega: the First and the Last (Revelation 1:8)

Jehovah-Rohi: the Lord our Shepherd (Psalm 23)

El Shaddai: the Almighty or the All Sufficient (Genesis 17:1)

Kadosh: the Holy One (Isaiah 40:25)

Abba: Father/Daddy (Romans 8:15)

Jehovah-Shalom: the Lord our Peace (Judges 6:24)

Prayer for Today:

Most Holy God, thank you that your names reveal so much about You. Thank you for being our loving Father, our Provider, our Peace, and all that we need. Amen

Training in Godliness

For physical training is of some value, but godliness has value for all things, holding promise for both the present life and the life to come.
1 Timothy 4:8

Have you ever observed how people will drive around in circles in a parking lot until a space opens up near the entrance of the store? This might make sense if the person is feeling weak, or if someone has many packages to carry. But I have even noticed this behavior in the parking lot at my local gym. It seems totally illogical to avoid walking 20 extra yards when your whole purpose for being at the gym is to get exercise!

The Bible gives some value to physical training, but spiritual exercise that leads to godliness has even more worth. Paul encouraged Timothy to develop in godliness, which *has value for all things, holding promise for both the present life and the life to come.* (1 Timothy 4:8). In his first letter to the Corinthian church, he compared spiritual training to the regimen of an Olympic athlete. *Everyone who competes in the games goes into strict training. They do it to get a crown that will not last, but we do it to get a crown that will last forever.* (1 Corinthians 9:25)

Spiritual exercise comes from careful study of the Scriptures. *All Scripture is God-breathed and is useful for*

23

teaching, rebuking, correcting, and training in righteousness.
(2 Timothy 3:16) It is more than merely listening to preachers or skimming over religious materials. While these method have merit, they are not the equivalent of dedicated training. It's important to search the Bible on your own, allowing time to ponder the verses, pray, and consider what changes you might need to make.

Prayer for Today:

Dear God, I want to increase in righteousness, and I know that this takes training. Help me to be self-disciplined, and give me a deep desire to grow more like You. Thank you that your Word is useful to teach and correct. May I be obedient to the truths that I discover in the Scriptures. Amen.

Planning Ahead

Now listen, you who say, "Today or tomorrow we will go to this or that city, spend a year there, carry on business and make money." Why, you do not even know what will happen tomorrow. What is your life? You are a mist that appears for a little while and then vanishes. Instead, you ought to say, "If it is the Lord's will, we will live and do this or that." As it is, you boast in your arrogant schemes. All such boasting is evil. James 4: 13-16

Campgrounds are filling up! With more and more people hitting the road, reservations at prime locations have to be made months in advance. I recently realized that I had l lost track of the reservation time frame required to sign up for a Corps of Engineers campground for a trip that was still five months away. There were literally zero out of 187 sites at this location available with any hookups. So much for the spontaneity of RV living!

In so many areas of life, we have to find a balance between planning ahead and keeping our options open. How can anyone know if the week that we have selected for our trip will be idyllic or filled with downpours? If I commit to attending this university, will I miss out on an even better experience elsewhere? Is the construction zone delay that has me so frustrated actually saving me from an encounter with a semi at an intersection down the road? Only God knows the end from the beginning: *"For I know the plans that I have for you,"* declares the Lord, *"plans to prosper you and not to harm you, plans to give you hope and a future."* (Jeremiah 29:11) The Bible encourages planning and hard work: *Lazy hands make for poverty, but diligent hands bring wealth.* (Proverbs 10:4) But we are also admonished to trust our future to God and remain sensitive to His leading. Our plans should not be a source of boasting or become idols that are more important than something new that He may place in our path.

Prayer for Today:

Dear Heavenly Father, you are the Eternal one. Every moment of my life was known by you before a single one took place. You love me so much, and you want to guide and direct my days. May all that I say and do be for your glory and for the good of myself and others. Amen.

Where's the Bread?

Jesus Christ is the same, yesterday and today and forever. Hebrews 13:8

Halfway through our camping trip, the time had come to stock up on fresh food, so we stopped at a small-town grocery store. I spent quite a long time wandering through the aisles because the store layout was totally unfamiliar to me. At home, I have frequented my three favorite grocery stores so many times that I know exactly how the various sections of each store are arranged. This store felt strange and somehow even disorganized. I craved the security of sameness.

Same does not have to equal boring. Sameness can lead to a feeling of security, because we know exactly what to expect. This is why children love to hear the same story over and over. Jesus does not change capriciously. He is the same, now and forevermore. His promises remain true, his love is constant, and his advice for a fulfilled life remain unchanged. No additional revelation or unique ideas are necessary to find the path to a relationship with God. *His divine power has given us everything we need for a godly life through our knowledge of him who called us by his own glory and goodness.* (2 Peter 1:3)

If I choose to wander aimlessly, distracted by the shiny baubles of novel philosophies that have no secure base, I will

27

end up wasting time or even losing my way. Jesus promises the deepest joy and the greatest future to those who follow the truth of his wise commands and rest in his eternal, unchanging grace.

Prayer for Today:

Dear Lord, you are unchanging, and you know what will lead to true joy. Thank you that I can always count on you. May I use your Word as the guiding path for my life. Amen.

Hypocritical Messages

The Lord says, "These people come near to me with their mouth and honor me with their lips, but their hearts are far from me." Isaiah 29:13

Isn't it fun to decipher personalized license plates? Some are pretty obvious in their meaning, such as ART LVR, THX GRMPS, or SMLE DOC. Others are much more obscure, because only the owners know the background stories that inspired them. As we travel, I often find myself reading the letters and numbers on license plates aloud, trying to unravel their messages. One thing is for sure, anyone whose plate proclaims love for God had better be a safe and courteous driver! If not, they send a hypocritical message to everyone on the road.

For several years, I had a bumper sticker for a Christian radio station on the back of my car. It was placed there mainly in the hope that anyone who drove behind me might tune in to the station numbers on the sticker and find the hope and truth of God. I soon realized that the sticker was a good reminder to myself that I needed to drive in a way that glorified God. Since I had taken the step of publicly identifying with Christ, I needed to honor Him with my actions.

I will never achieve perfection, but I need to "practice what what I preach". My actions must be in alignment with my proclamation in order to avoid being rightly denounced as a hypocrite. Taking it one step further, if the inner attitudes of my heart don't correspond to my proclamation, I am equally at fault before God. The psalmist wisely prayed, *May these words of my mouth and this meditation of my heart be pleasing in your sight, Lord, my Rock and my Redeemer.* (Psalm 19:14)

Prayer for Today:

My gracious Lord, I want to identify with You without being a hypocrite. I rely on your help in order to obey your commands. Thank you that you forgive sins and purify hearts. Amen.

Tree of Life

A soothing tongue is a tree of life, but a perverse tongue crushes the spirit. Proverbs 15:4

A winter stroll can provide lovely views of deciduous trees with bare branches. Winter trees don't usually get as much admiration as their showy autumn counterparts, but they are still beautiful and very much alive. In the Bible, the tree is often used as a symbol of abundant life. The psalmist describes the man who meditates on the God's law as being *like a tree planted by streams of water, which yields its fruit in season.* (Psalm 1:3) The Book of Revelation has many references to the tree of life which grows in the celestial city. *Blessed are those who wash their robes, that they may have the right to the tree of life and may go through the gates into the city.* (Revelation 22:14)

The Book of Proverbs includes four different metaphors associated with a tree of life: wisdom (Proverbs 3:13,18), the fruit of the righteous (Proverbs 11:30), a longing fulfilled (Proverbs 13:12), and a soothing tongue (Proverbs 15:4). A soothing tongue is presented as being the opposite of a perverse tongue which crushes the spirit. Speech that degrades another person truly does yield a crushing emotional blow. It's never really accurate to say, "Sticks and stones may break my bones, but words will never hurt me." Words have consequences,

31

and Scripture affirms the life-giving power of a soothing tongue.

Who has God placed in your path today that needs to be healed by your gracious words? Let your wise, righteous, soothing words bring life.

Prayer for Today:

Dear God, my tongue often causes me to sin.
Please help me to grow in my ability to control
my speech. If you place me in a situation
today where I can provide soothing words,
may I not squander the opportunity to give life.

Bear with Each Other

Therefore, as God's chosen people, holy and dearly loved, clothe yourselves with compassion, kindness, humility, gentleness and patience. Bear with each other and forgive one another if any of you has a grievance against someone. Forgive as the Lord forgave you. And over all these virtues put on love, which binds them all together in perfect unity. Let the peace of Christ rule in your hearts, since as members of one body you were called to peace. And be thankful. Colossians 3:12-15

Perhaps you have seen the T shirt design that says, "Sorry for what I said when we were backing up the camper." The humor in that slogan is tinged with a measure of truth. We've all experienced stressful conversations while maneuvering into particularly tricky campsites. On our second trip with our new travel trailer, we quickly discovered why our site had been the only one available for that beautiful fall weekend. A tightly curved, narrow road with bushes on one side and trees on the other, the rutted gravel driveway, and the rise in the road that made it necessary to "gun" the engine to even back up – you get the picture. After many attempts under the watchful eye of some curious but gracious neighbors, we finally accomplished our goal without any harsh words.

When Paul reminds the Colossians to "bear with each other", he is not advocating gritting our teeth, rolling our eyes, and repeating the shortcomings of the other person under our breath. The surrounding verses provide a context of love, humility, patience, and forgiveness. When we are humble, we don't assume that we always know best. When we think and speak in love, we regard as important the feelings of others. Patience enables us to take a deep breath and work through a problem. The peace of Christ leads to unity and thankfulness.

Prayer for Today:

Almighty God, help me to remember that you
have shown grace to me. May I treat others
with honor, patience, and love in all the
situations which I experience this day. Amen.

Mosquito Magnet

Nebuchadnezzar then approached the opening of the blazing furnace and shouted, "Shadrach, Meshach, and Abednego, servants of the Most High God, come out! Come here!" So Shadrach, Meshach, and Abednego came out of the fire, and the satraps, prefects, governors and royal advisers crowded around them. They saw that the fire had not harmed their bodies, nor was a hair of their heads singed; their robes were not scorched, and there was no smell of fire on them. Daniel 3: 26-27

Have you noticed that mosquitos really prefer some people to others? Scientists attribute the preference of these blood-suckers to many factors. Some we can't control, such as the chemical composition of our skin or our blood type (condolences to all you type O campers!) But there are a few actions we can take to become less of a mosquito magnet. Wear light colored clothing, stay indoors at dawn and dusk, and avoid drinking excess alcohol. The other obvious strategy is to spray on oily, smelly repellant. This is effective, but the scent is is an obnoxious clue to others that we have applied bug spray. In the same way, if it will be obvious to others that we have been tending a campfire when our hair and clothes take on that distinctive, smoky smell.

When Shadrach, Meshach, and Abednego emerged from the fiery furnace after being rescued by God, King Nebuchadnezzar and his entourage were astounded. Not only had the three men escaped the king's horrific death sentence, but there was virtually no evidence that they had ever been exposed to the flames. Their bodies were unharmed, their head unsinged, their robes unscorched, and no smell of fire remained on them. The Creator had overcome the laws of creation and protected them from all effects of the fire. Truly, *all things are possible with God!* (Mark 10:27)

The response of Nebuchadnezzar to this miracle was to voice praise to the one true God and to require all the people to worship only Him. He also commended Shadrach, Meshach, and Abednego for their trust in God and their willingness to give up their lives rather than betray their beliefs. The three men were then promoted to higher positions in the province of Babylon. We may not receive a similar promotion at the workplace when we remain true to the Lord, but honoring God will always bring spiritual benefits.

Prayer for Today:

Dear Heavenly Father, you are pleased when we trust in you and remain faithful. You have the power to rescue us so completely that even the stench of evil cannot remain on us. May I continue to follow you in such a way that those around me will see your almighty ability to do the impossible and give praise to you. Amen.

Meet me on the Road

They asked each other, "Were our hearts not burning within us while he talked with us on the road and opened the Scriptures to us?" Luke 24:32

After the crucifixion, Cleopas and another disciple were walking to the village of Emmaus, their hearts heavy with grief and disappointment. Jesus came along side them and joined their journey, but they did not recognize him. The men told him that the prophet whom they had followed had been crucified, and they stated their skepticism about reports of the resurrection. Jesus, still unrecognizable to them, began to explain in detail the Scriptures concerning the Messiah. Upon arriving at their destination, he joined them for a meal, and at this time their eyes were opened to recognize the risen Christ. The two men asked each other, *Were not our hearts burning within us while he talked with us on the road and opened the Scriptures to us?* (Luke 24:32)

Filled with joy, the two then ran to tell the news of their amazing experience to more disciples. The larger group had barely finished hearing their account when Christ miraculously stood in their midst. Jesus reassured them that he was truly alive, explained the Scriptures to all who were present, promised to send the Holy Spirit, blessed them, and finally was taken up into heaven. Can you imagine the exhilaration and

37

exhaustion of the two men at the end of that day? The morning had begun with a long journey and a dearth of hope. The evening had closed with the assurance that Jesus was indeed the Messiah. The one in whom they had placed their faith and trust was worthy of their worship. In between, the day had brought a new understanding of the Scriptures that would transform their lives and remain with them going forward.

We cannot physically travel down the road with Jesus as he explains the Word to us, but the Holy Spirit can be our teacher. If we continue to read and meditate upon the Scriptures, we will understand them more and more. We can find forgiveness and grace when we fall short. If we seek God, He will be with us on every road.

Prayer for Today:

Dear Lord, you met the two men on the road to Emmaus and brought hope to them. You explained the truth of the Scriptures and gave them understanding. Each day, help me to remember that your Holy Spirit can give me insight into your Word. Thank you that your grace is available to bring forgiveness and your presence will never abandon me. You are my hope and my peace. Amen.

Press On

I want to know Christ-yes, to know the power of his resurrection and participation in his sufferings, becoming like him in his death, and so, somehow, attaining to the resurrection from the dead... Brothers and sisters, I do not consider myself yet to have taken hold of it. But one thing I do: Forgetting what is behind and straining toward what is ahead, I press on toward the goal to win the prize for which God has called me heavenward in Christ Jesus. Philippians 3: 10, 13-15

Long hiking trails that lead to an overlook or a summit are often "out and back" trails rather than loops. When weariness sets in, it's tempting to turn around before reaching the peak, yet reversing course seems like a poor option because you will miss the main destination of the hike. If you are able to press on, the goal can usually be achieved, and the reward is a breathtaking view.

In his letter to the believers at Philippi, Paul spoke of pressing on toward a heavenly goal – that of knowing Christ, experiencing both the power of the resurrection and the suffering that comes with identification with Him. Times of difficulty and persecution can cause us to seek easier paths, but pressing on leads to power for living today and progress toward our promised heavenly home. Like Paul, we must forget the failures of the past and strain toward future growth. When our goal is to know Christ, the rewards along the journey are a foretaste of the rewards of the destination.

Prayer for Today:

Dear Lord, the journey which I began with you leads heavenward. Please forgive my shortcomings and help me to leave them behind. Grant me resolve and focus as I strain hard toward the goal of knowing you. Thank you that you promise strength and wisdom to those who walk your paths. Amen.

All the Power We Need

May the God of hope fill you with all joy and peace as you trust in him, so that you may overflow with hope by the power of the Holy Spirit. Romans 15:13

Choosing a tow vehicle with sufficient power is a complicated math puzzle. Gross weight/tongue weight/payload capacity – on and on go the calculations. Some owners hope to save money or prefer a smaller vehicle for non-camping days, so they tow with something that has barely enough power to pull their rig. Others say, "Bring out the big trucks!" and love the confidence that owning a heavy-duty tow vehicle can bring. Most owners realize that safety demands a certain level of power for pulling up an incline or braking down a hill.

The Holy Spirit is our source of spiritual power. Christ promised that the Holy Spirit would indwell every believer. Immediately before ascending into heaven, he told the disciples, *you will receive power when the Holy Spirit comes on you, and you will be my witnesses in Jerusalem, and in all Judea and Samaria, and to the ends of the earth.* (Acts 1:8) The disciples were also encouraged by Jesus to ask for the Holy Spirit: *If you then, though you are evil, know how to give good gifts to your children, how much more will your Father in heaven give the Holy Spirit to those who ask him!* (Luke

11:13). The filling of the Spirit enabled the believers to speak boldly for Christ and to display the fruits of the Spirit: *And the disciples were filled with joy and with the Holy Spirit.* (Acts 13:52) *But the fruit of the Spirit is love, joy, peace, forbearance, kindness, goodness, faithfulness, gentleness and self-control.* (Galatians 5:22-23)

Without the Spirit's power, we can't accomplish God's will, and we are left vulnerable to temptation and discouragement. Each day, remind yourself that your own strength and wisdom are insufficient. Specifically ask God for the promised indwelling, enabling guidance of the Holy Spirit in your life.

Prayer for Today:

Heavenly Father, you know what challenges lie ahead this day. May I not rely on my own wisdom and strength. Fill me with the power of your Holy Spirit, Amen.

An Easy Yoke

Come to me, all you who are weary and burdened, and I will give you rest. Take my yoke upon you and learn from me, for I am gentle and humble in heart, and you will find rest for your souls. For my yoke is easy and my burden is light. Matthew 11:28-30

I enjoyed backpacking in high school with a group of Explorer Scouts. This group deliberately avoided the most heavily traveled trails and sought out less crowded destinations. Along with our sponsor/chaperone, we would park along the road at a trailhead somewhere near the Skyline Drive. The first day we would descend through the forest until we found a good place to camp at the bottom of a gorge near a water source. The second day was much tougher as we had no choice but to ascend on and on until we arrived back at our cars. The shared joke was always, "Where's the helicopter pickup?" No chopper ever appeared, so we would arrive at the vehicles totally exhausted, more than ready to be released from the burden of our backpacks.

Jesus promised rest for the weary and burdened, but his prescription was surprising. We are to take a yoke upon our shoulders and learn from him. A yoke usually refers to a heavy wooden bar used to connect a pair of oxen so that the team can jointly pull a plow. It can also refer to a device that would be put upon the neck of a defeated person. The yoke generally had a negative connotation of oppression, such as *under the yoke of the Egyptians* (Exodus 6:6) and *My father laid on you a heavy yoke.*(1 Kings 12:11) But Jesus promised that his yoke is easy and his burden is light. When we learn from Him, our souls find rest.

What are some practical ways that we can do this? We come to Jesus daily by being physically, mentally, and spiritually still, placing the activities and concerns of the day before him and leaving them there. We learn from Jesus by studying the Scriptures before listening to any preacher. We can yoke ourselves to Christ, moving in the same direction and at the same pace as the Savior, by obeying His commands.

Prayer for Today:

Dear Jesus, I come to you today and leave my
burdens with you. May I follow your
commands today, and may the work that I do
be in coordination with your Word. Please
help me to rest completely in You. Amen.

Armor Checklist

Finally, be strong in the Lord and in his mighty power. Put on the full armor of God, so that you can take your stand against the devil's schemes. For our struggle is not against flesh and blood, but against the rulers, against the authorities, against the powers of this dark world and against the spiritual forces of evil in the heavenly realms. Therefore put on the full armor of God, so that when the day of evil comes, you may be able to stand your ground, and after you have done everything, to stand. Stand firm then, with the belt of truth buckled around your waist, with the breastplate of righteousness in place, and with your feet fitted with the readiness that comes from the gospel of peace. In addition to all this, take up the shield of faith, with which you can extinguish all the flaming arrows of the evil one. Take the helmet of salvation and the sword of the Spirit, which is the word of God. Ephesians 6:10-17

I need checklists! For camping trips, we have checklists for packing, unhitching/setting up, hitching/preparing to travel, yearly maintenance, and more. Checklists have saved us from heading down the road with the glass plate jangling around in the microwave or with cabinets not securely latched. We've been saved from leaving behind essential food or gear. Most importantly, we've been saved from neglecting tasks that are critical for safety on the road.

Paul provided a checklist for the believers in the city of Ephesus in order to provide them with protection from the spiritual forces of evil that are present in the world. He used a metaphor which would have been very familiar to them: the suit of armor worn by the Roman soldiers who occupied their land. Each piece of the armor was designed to help the soldier stand firm in battle. Meditate on the armor of God and use it as your checklist each morning to lead you to victory over spiritual darkness.

Belt of truth: John 8:32 *Then you will know the truth, and the truth will set you free.*
Breastplate of righteousness: Romans 3:22 *This righteousness is given through faith in Jesus Christ to all who believe.*
Shoes of the gospel of peace: Acts 10:36 *You know the message God sent to the people of Israel, announcing the good news of peace through Jesus Christ, who is Lord of all.*
Shield of faith: Hebrews 11:1 *Now faith is confidence in what we hope for and assurance about what we do not see.*
Helmet of salvation: Acts 4:12 *Salvation is found in no one else, for there is no other name under heaven given to mankind by which we must be saved.*
Sword of the spirit/the word of God: Luke 11:28 *Blessed rather are those who hear the word of God and obey it.*

Prayer for Today:

Mighty God, the victory is ultimately yours,
and you have given me special armor in order
to push back against evil. May I consciously
use each of these pieces of provision that come
with empowerment from you. Amen.

Red Light Justice

The sins of some are obvious, reaching the place of judgment ahead of them; the sins of others trail behind them. In the same way, good deeds are obvious, and even those that are not obvious cannot remain hidden forever. 1 Timothy 5:24-25

"Where are the police when you need them?" I muttered to myself as a car barreled through a red light ahead of me, endangering everyone in the intersection. Many states and towns have installed red light cameras, and this has caused at least some drivers to think twice before heading through a red light. But the cameras are controversial in some areas and have been banned in many states due to legal issues. Regardless of whether or not a person receives a ticket, their infraction is obvious to anyone nearby and their misdeed is viewed by God. Other traffic "sins" are less obvious, such as distracted driving while adjusting the radio or munching chips, and these actions can also lead to an accident.

Numbers 32:23 warns, *you may be sure that your sin will find you out.* Proverbs 28:13 gives this reminder: *Whoever conceals their sins does not prosper, but the one who confesses and renounces them finds mercy.*

When I see others engage in blatant sin, there's nothing wrong with wishing that justice will prevail. Yet I need to recognize that I am certainly not without sin myself. Introspection should be based on God's Word, and this self-assessment will lead to confession, mercy, and humility.

Prayer for Today:

Dear Heavenly Father, like the psalmist I humbly make my prayer to you. *Wash away all my iniquity and cleanse me from my sin.* May I never display a "holier than thou" arrogance. Show me the areas in which my outward deeds or inner thoughts are not pleasing to you. Give me a resolve to change, and thank you for your unfailing grace and mercy. Amen.

The Heavens Declare

The heavens declare the glory of God; the skies proclaim the work of his hands. Day after day they pour forth speech; night after night they reveal knowledge. Psalm 19:1-2

Someday I hope to visit a Dark Sky Park, an exceptionally dark site designated by the International Dark-Sky Association in which there is minimal light pollution, allowing for amazing star-gazing. Psalm 19 tells us that the heavens are on display in order to declare the glory of God. What specifically can the heavens reveal about God?

God is awesome. The size of the universe is beyond our ability to comprehend. We are only infinitesimal specks in the cosmos. *When I consider your heavens, the work of your fingers, the moon and the stars, which you have set in place, what is mankind that you are mindful of them?" (Psalm 8:3-4)*

God is orderly. Even early civilizations were able to track the heavenly bodies through their predictable paths. *As long as the earth endures, seedtime and harvest, cold and heat, summer and winter, day and night will never cease."* (Genesis 8:22)

God is creative. The creativity of God is on display throughout the universe. Planets, stars, comets, meteors – all reveal the fascinating breadth of God's inventive hand. Each star (like each snowflake and each person) is unique. *Lift up your eyes and look to the heavens: Who created all these? He who brings out the starry host one by one and calls forth each of them by name."* (Isaiah 40:26)

God is loving. His creation provides all that we need. Just as we are designed to need the Sun for warmth and for our food supply, we also need the universe to fulfill our soul's longing for beauty. *Give thanks to the Lord of lords: His love endures forever. To him who alone does great wonders, His love endures forever. Who by his understanding made the heavens, His love endures forever."* (Psalm 136:3-5)

Prayer for Today:

Dear God, the heavens declare your glory. Thank you for providing a clear message to all mankind of your awesome power and creativity. Thank you that we can depend on the orderliness of your creation and the constancy of your love and mercy. Amen.

Strong as Eggs?

For you have been my refuge, a strong tower against the foe. Psalm
61:3

Molded fiberglass travel trailers are often called eggs, and
there are a number of egg camper rallies available for those
who enjoy socializing with like-minded owners. Fiberglass
camper owners like myself tend to be very loyal, and the
trailers hold their value well due to fewer water leaks and their
strong, smooth finish.

The eggshells of birds can be both brittle and strong. One
reason that a hen can sit on her eggs without breaking them is
that the dome shape of the "pointy" end of each egg evenly
distributes her weight. If the eggs were on their sides in the
nest, they would be more apt to break under the pressure of the
hen's body.   The egg is a perfectly protective refuge in which
the bird can safely grow and develop.

The Bible refers to God as both a refuge and a strong
tower. Although the world around us is swirling with turmoil,
the Lord wants us to rest safely in Him. Just as He provides
food for the birds, loveliness for the lilies, and protection for
developing eggs, He will take care of us. Just as He calls each
star by name, we are individually known and loved. Our part is

to be still, to remember His blessings and provision, to bring our needs before Him in prayer, and to place our trust in Him.

Prayer for Today:

Dear God, you are our loving Heavenly Father. You have designed the perfect refuge for baby chicks, and you care for me as well. Please help me to cast off worry and to trust in you as my refuge and my strong tower. Amen.

Taking a Toll

And whoever does not carry their cross and follow me cannot be my disciple. Suppose one of you wants to build a tower. Won't you first sit down and estimate the cost to see if you have enough money to complete it? Luke 14: 27-28

On a journey through an unfamiliar area, we once encountered a toll road that we were not expecting. There was no way to avoid getting on the road from our current position on the ramp, and instead of a booth with a human attendant, there was only a mechanical bin into which coins needed to be dropped. Many dollars worth of coins! This exorbitant fee left us desperately searching for spare change in the folds of our seats and in our backpacks. After scraping together barely enough money for the toll, we entered the highway and immediately looked for the next exit. There was no way that we could afford another toll booth further down the road, so we were forced to find a new highway. If we had only known about the toll ahead of time, we would have counted the cost and made an informed decision about our route.

Jesus admonished his disciples to count the cost of following him. The price was clear: they were to carry their cross. In the time of Christ, if you saw a person carrying a cross, you could be certain that the individual was on his way to die. Many of the original disciples ultimately died as martyrs. They also died figuratively while serving Christ on Earth as they abandoned their sinful habits, their personal ambitions, and their human comforts in order to follow Jesus.

There is a cost to following Jesus today. The persecuted church around the world is demonstrating for us what it means to count the cost and make a decision to fully follow Christ. The reward is as clear as the price. *Be faithful, even to the point of death, and I will give you life as your victor's crown. (Revelation 2:10)*

Prayer for Today:

Dear God, I want to follow Christ completely. I understand that following him has a cost, so please help me to be faithful, even unto death if necessary. Thank you that you have promised to send your presence to strengthen and encourage me. Please grant grace to those who are facing severe persecution. May all who identify as your disciples be found faithful. Amen.

Chasing 70

As long as the earth endures, seedtime and harvest, cold and heat, summer and winter, day and night will never cease. (Genesis 8:22)

Are you "chasing 70", keeping on the move in order to avoid temperature extremes and remain in 70 degree weather? While I can see the appeal of this concept, I also really enjoy living in an area that experiences all four seasons. I might not want to camp for long in extreme cold or heat, but I am thankful for the variety and the loveliness of each part of the year. Many countries have only two seasons: rainy and dry. You can be sure that if I lived in one of those nations, I'd be "chasing dry"! But farmers would likely prefer to have a balance.

After the flood, Noah and his family left the ark, along with the animals. Noah offered sacrifices of thanks to God, and God promised never again to send a flood that would cover the whole earth. He also promised that there would be a reliable progression of seasons as long as the earth endures. (Genesis 8:22)

Because the seasons are so reliable, they are often used in Scripture to illustrate important truths. In the Book of James, a person who patiently waits for the second coming of Jesus is compared to a farmer who *waits for the land to yield its valuable crop, patiently waiting for the autumn and spring rains.* (James 5:7)   Jesus himself used a seasonal metaphor to describe the signs of his approaching return. *Now learn this lesson from the fig tree: As soon as its twigs get tender and its leaves come out, you know that summer is near. Even so, when you see these things happening, you know that it is near, right at the door.* (Mark 13:28) The Book of Amos describes a time of coming judgement for the wealthy who live in multiple seasonal homes and worship idols: *"On the day I punish Israel for her sins, I will destroy the altars of Bethel; the horns of the altar will be cut off and fall to the ground. I will tear down the winter house along with the summer house; the houses adorned with ivory will be destroyed and the mansions will be demolished" declares the Lord.* (Amos 3:14-15)

The predictable course of the seasons is caused by the intricate movements of celestial bodies. Our awesome God has given the seasons to us as a blessing and as a sign of his reliability and faithfulness. What should be our response? We can say along with the psalmist, *Teach me your way, Lord, that I may rely on your faithfulness; give me an undivided heart, that I may fear your name.* (Psalm 86:11)

Prayer for Today:

Dear Lord, every season that you have made is filled with beauty. Each one is a testimony to your power, creativity, and consistent faithfulness. When Jesus returns to the earth according to your promise, may I be found patiently waiting, growing in purity, and doing your will.

Eunice

I am reminded of your sincere faith, which first lived in your grandmother Lois and in your mother Eunice and, I am persuaded, now lives in you also. 2 Timothy 1:5

Do you know anyone named Eunice? It's certainly not one of more popular female Bible names such as Sarah or Elizabeth. Eunice derives from a Greek word that means *good victory*. In the United States, it peaked in popularity in the year 1910 and is memorable for Eunice Harper Higgins, a fictional character on The Carol Burnett Show, and Eunice Kennedy Shriver, founder of the Special Olympics. Only one verse in Scripture mentions anyone named Eunice. Paul observes that Eunice, the mother of Timothy, and Lois, Timothy's grandmother, both possessed a sincere faith that also lived in Timothy himself.

Salvation cannot be inherited. We are not genuine believers merely because our relatives were followers of Christ. Each individual must make their own decision to believe in the saving work of Christ on their behalf. But parents and grandparents obviously have a profound effect on our lives as they faithfully (or unfaithfully) live out the Gospel before us on a daily basis, in good times and bad. I would love to have spent a few days with the extended family of Timothy to learn from them, and I pray that my children and grandchildren will be drawn closer to God through their interactions with me.

What are some keys to having a positive spiritual influence on our children, grandchildren, nieces and nephews, and the children in our church or neighborhood that God has put in our path?

Pray specifically for each one by name. Pray for their faith journey, and ask God to equip you and others to be positive examples of the transforming power of God.

Speak of your faith in an open and genuine way, interjecting truth into casual conversations rather than sermonizing.

Apologize when you have hurt their feelings or made errors in judgement.

Look for creative ways to show love and care, not just by giving physical presents.

Display the joy of the Lord. Following Christ is not a dreary way to live!

Prayer for Today:

Father, you have placed children in my path that are watching my life. May I honor you in all my interactions with them. May they come to possess a sincere faith, and may they grow in the grace and knowledge of you. Amen.

Grill Master

How many are your works, Lord! In wisdom you made them all; the earth is full of your creatures. There is the sea, vast and spacious, teeming with creatures beyond number - living things both large and small. There the ships go to and fro, and Leviathan, which you formed to frolic there. All creatures look to you to give them their food at the proper time. Psalm 104:24-27

Cooking while camping: let me count the ways! Some families pull out elaborate grills and sear mouth-watering steaks and kebabs that are the envy of their neighbors. Others enjoy more budget-friendly options, such as hot dogs and s'mores. I like to freeze ahead at least three days worth of main dishes that can be quickly reheated. This way, for the first few days of a trip, I can spend more time hiking and less time cooking. Whatever your style, most people prefer not to eat the same foods day after day. Variety is the spice of life.

God has given us a huge variety of fruits, vegetables, and other foods to eat, and we have been provided with creative brains with which to mix and match them together in innumerable ways. It is estimated that there are over 4,000 types of potatoes around the globe. Some foods that we might be reluctant to eat are a dietary staple for people in other parts of the world. And still other foods provide perfect nutrition for animals. Every creature has been provided for by our wise Creator.

There are many ways to properly respond to these truths. Thankfulness for the provision of our needs. Generosity to share with the hungry. Joy in appreciating delicious foods. Amazement that the God of the myriad stars and the myriad potatoes and the myriad types of people takes notice of me as an individual.

Prayer for Today:

Dear God, your awesome power and creativity
are evident everywhere. Thank you that you
have provided for my needs in every way.
May I be generous to share so that no one you
have created will go hungry. I am so blessed to
be personally known and loved by you. Amen.

Haste Makes Waste

The plans of the diligent lead to profit as surely as haste leads to poverty. Proverbs 21:5
Do you see someone who speaks in haste? There is more hope for a fool than for them. Proverbs 29:20

Have you ever had a "haste makes waste" moment? Most of us have experienced far too many of these situations. We try to do something in a rush, only to end up wasting even more time trying to undo the results of our haste. At home, this might involve racing around the kitchen to speed up breakfast, only to clumsily knock a jar of jelly onto the floor. On the road, haste could lead to catastrophe if we attempt to squeeze through that yellow light or try to drive away from a campsite without properly hitching to our tow vehicle.

The Book of Proverbs has some interesting lessons to teach about haste in work and in speech. Haste is contrasted with diligent planning. We are less likely to exceed the speed limit in the morning if we set out everything that we need for work or school the previous night. Planning also helps prevent haphazard actions that are counter productive, such as being forced to purchase items on the road that don't really suit our needs in the long run.

Hasty speech is condemned throughout Scripture. *Everyone should be quick to listen, slow to speak and slow to become angry, because human anger does not produce the righteousness that God desires.* (James 1:19-20) I can't count the number of times that I have spoken words in haste that I have regretted. Saying "I'm sorry" doesn't completely undo the hurt or misunderstanding that has been caused. A quick response on social media can be equally harmful. *A gentle answer turns away wrath, but a harsh word stirs up anger. The tongue of the wise adorns knowledge, but the mouth of the fool gushes folly.* (Proverbs 15:1-2)

The next time you are tempted to act or speak in haste, remind yourself that haste makes waste.

Prayer for Today:

Dear God, I often act or speak in haste. Help me to be wise and disciplined in planning so that I can avoid harmful or wasteful actions. Give me self-control over my tongue, and make me a more sincere listener. Amen.

The First One There

It has always been my ambition to preach the gospel where Christ was not known, so that I would not be building on someone else's foundation. Romans 15:20

When I travel to a beautiful natural location such as Grand Tetons National Park or Niagara Falls, I often wonder what it would have been like to be one of the first humans to see that incredible place. No crowds of tourists, only silence and an awe-inspiring view. News would quickly spread far and wide about the spot, because nothing that amazing can be kept a secret for long. But until the crowds arrived, the first ones there could enjoy their wonderful discovery.

Now contrast that image with one of a new neighborhood under construction. I walk several times a week in one of these subdivisions, filled with the clamor of hammers and dump trucks as more and more homes are built. For months, even though several of the homes had seemed complete, no one had actually moved in. I kept wondering if the developer was waiting until a certain date so that several families would move in at about the same time. After all, who wants to be the only family in the middle of a construction zone? At least if there are several residents they can become friends and share common interests. Eventually, one brave family took possession of their sparkling new home, pioneers in the suburbs.

Finally, consider what it is like when a small group of missionaries enters a crowded, noisy city, knowing that there are few others who share their beliefs. Daily they hear the sounds of unfamiliar languages and the calls to prayer from other religions. They are the first ones there from their sending organization, homesick and needing much wisdom going forward. But they are determined to persevere because they have a message of hope for that city.

It's so important to pray for international workers as they navigate new and uncomfortable situations. Pray also about situations that God may be opening up for you in which you will need to be the first one to step forward with the light of life. This step might involve calling someone, offering hope or an apology, sending an email to a person that you don't know very well, perhaps feeling a bit sheepish or awkward. If God is prompting your heart, be the first one there.

Prayer for Today:

Dear Lord, there are many today who are living in difficult and lonely places and who seek to share your hope and grace. Bless and encourage them this day. Help me to step forward into the unknown to serve you, according to your leading. Amen.

Downsizing for Contentment

For we brought nothing into the world, and we can take nothing out of it. But if we have food and clothing, we will be content with that.
1 Timothy 6:7-9

Downsizing for full-time RV living is a massive undertaking, but once the stress of the initial purge has passed, simplicity can actually reduce stress. Even part-time travelers often find that they need fewer and fewer items on board as time goes on. Minimalists point out that every possession you own has to be purchased, maintained, stored, and eventually disposed of. The Bible says, *godliness with contentment is great gain.* (1 Timothy 6:6) Let's discover some other bits of wisdom regarding contentment and how to acquire it.

Hebrews 13:5 *Keep your lives free from the love of money and be content with what you have, because God has said, "Never will I leave you; never will I forsake you."* Contentment springs from avoiding the love of money and remembering that God will never leave or forsake me.

Psalm 131:2 *But I have calmed and quieted myself, I am like a weaned child with its mother; like a weaned child I am content.*

Contentment can be fostered by consciously being still and seeking calm.

Philippians 4:12-13 *I know what it is to be in need, and I know what it is to have plenty. I have learned the secret of being content in any and every situation, whether well fed or hungry, whether living in plenty or in want. I can do all this through him who gives me strength.* Experience is a good teacher. It's helpful to remember that God has always been with us and will continue to strengthen us.

Prayer for Today:

Dear Heavenly Father, You alone can bring contentment of the mind and the soul. Help me to be satisfied with my possessions and content in my current situation. May I remember your past provision and rest in the peace that you grant to those who seek you. Amen.

Stones of Remembrance

And Joshua set up at Gilgal the twelve stones they had taken out of the Jordan. He said to the Israelites, "In the future when your descendants ask their parents, 'What do these stones mean?' tell them, 'Israel crossed the Jordan on dry ground.'" Joshua 4:20-22

Do you collect stones or seashells? Picking up unique items from outdoor walks is a habit that begins as a toddler. Many a mother has discovered a rock or acorn tumbling along with her child's blue jeans in the clothes dryer. A town nature park near my home has set up a special acrylic box so that children will learn to put their treasures in the box as they leave the trail, rather than removing them from the park. On my first visit to the Pacific Northwest, I was so taken with the smooth burgundy, grey, and mauve stones on the beach that I hauled a large baggie of them home to display in a bowl. Perhaps I should have heeded the popular expression often attributed to Chief Seattle: "Leave only footprints/take only memories."

Some people are so intent upon preserving memories of a place through photographs that they are unable to enjoy the actual experience. Others spend excessive time or money in park gift shops. In addition to taking a few pictures of our own, our family's tradition is to purchase one photo magnet from each national park that we visit, a small but sufficient reminder of a treasured adventure.

When the children of Israel miraculously crossed over the Jordan River on dry ground, they were commanded to pick up twelve stones from the center of the river bed. These boulders became a memorial, stones of remembrance that would serve as continuing evidence of God's mighty power and faithfulness. They were more than just souvenirs. The rocks were sturdy and tangible reminders of a miracle. The chronicles of God' s powerful deeds were to be repeated over and over to each new generation of children who would someday view the stones.

Prayer for Today:

Dear Lord, the generation that comes after me needs to hear of your great deeds and faithful provision. May I take seriously my responsibility to pass on the truth of all that you have done in my life and in the lives of others. Amen.

Running the Gauntlet

The Sovereign Lord is my strength; he makes my feet like the feet of a deer, he enables me to tread on the heights. Habakkuk 3:19

The county in which I live is rapidly developing, with new neighborhoods sprouting up seemingly overnight. Wildlife native to this area is being pushed into a smaller and smaller territory as their woodland habitat shrinks. One result is that deer are often seen feeding in backyards, strolling on golf courses, and bounding across roads. Members of our family have had several collisions with deer on a particular section of road not far from our home. We refer to the experience of driving along this section as "running the gauntlet". Stress levels rise as our eyes dart back and forth across the road, looking for the slightest motion that could signal a deer starting a reckless leap into our path. Fortunately, none of our skirmishes with deer have resulted in personal injury, but the vehicles and the deer have not fared as well.

Deer are most active at dawn and dusk. They have good night vision, can live in rugged terrain, and have the ability to jump over eight feet high. The prophet Habakkuk rejoiced in prayer that because the Lord was his strength, he was enabled to tread on the heights securely, as a deer. This is a wonderful promise that is often quoted. But if you look at the context of the promise, the statements of confidence and trust are preceded by the pleading of the prophet.

Habakkuk implores God to repeat in his lifetime the awesome deeds of the past. *Lord I have heard of your fame; I stand in awe of your deeds, Lord. Repeat them in our day, in our time make them known; in wrath remember mercy. (Habakkuk 3:1-2)*

Habakkuk is facing the real possibility of an invasion by a marauding nation. He believes that God will send calamity on that nation, but he recognizes that God's rescue may not be immediate. *I heard and my heart pounded, my lips quivered at the sound; decay crept into my bones, and my legs trembled. Yet I will wait patiently for the day of calamity to come on the nation invading us. (Habakkuk 3:16)*

Finally, Habakkuk expresses a heart attitude that would be impossible to replicate without the Lord's power working within: *Though the fig tree does not bud and there are no grapes on the vines, though the olive crop fails and the fields produce no food, though there are no sheep in the pen and no cattle in the stalls, yet I will rejoice in the Lord, I will be joyful in God my Savior.* (Habakkuk 3:17-18)

Prayer for Today:

Dear Heavenly Father, you were with Habakkuk in his time of need, and you are also with me now. May I remember how you have worked mightily in the past for the nation of Israel and for individuals. You are the same yesterday, today, and forever. Give me a heart of rejoicing each day, and enable me, like a bounding deer, to tread on the heights. Amen.

Keeping Level

The path of the righteous is level; you, the Upright One, make the way of the righteous smooth. Isaiah 26:7

Leveling our trailer started off as a pretty basic process. Along with the small level built into our rig, we carried along a carpenter's bubble level, put it on the floor, and then made our adjustments. We later invested in a wireless vehicle leveling system which allowed us to monitor the process while parking the trailer. This simplified things immensely. At first, it seemed to me that having the trailer totally level wasn't really that critical. I had survived many years of backpacking trips and tent camping in less than flat conditions and had slept just fine. Then I learned that a propane RV refrigerator needs to be level within 1 or 2 degrees or it will not function properly and will quickly suffer damage.

Psalm 143:10 is a good example of how the concept of being level is presented in the Bible. *Teach me to do your will, for you are my God; may your good Spirit lead me on level ground.* In Jeremiah 31:9, the Israelite nation is promised, *I will lead them beside streams of water on a level path where they will not stumble.* In Isaiah 26:7, we read *The path of the righteous is level; you, the Upright One, make the way of the righteous smooth.* This does not mean that the Israelites will

71

not encounter setbacks and difficulties; rather it shows that God will guide them and lead them on the paths that are optimal for them. The prerequisite for this guidance is learning to do the will of God and living in righteousness. It is the path of the righteous that is level.

Enjoy these promises for those who follow the path of the righteous:

Proverbs 4:18 *The path of the righteous is like the morning sun, shining ever brighter till the full light of day.*
Proverbs 12:28 *In the way of righteousness there is life; along that path is immortality.*
Psalm 1:6 *For the Lord watches over the way of the righteous, but the way of the wicked leads to destruction.*

But if we all sin, how can we be declared righteous?

Romans 1:17 *For in the gospel the righteousness of God is revealed – a righteousness that is by faith from first to last, just as it is written: "The righteous will live by faith."*
Romans 3:22 *This righteousness is given through faith in Jesus Christ to all who believe.*

Prayer for Today:

Holy Father, you are righteous, and I am sinful. Thank you that because of Christ's sacrificial death on my behalf, I can be declared righteous and forgiven in your sight. I want to live in righteousness and holiness. Please lead me on level paths as I study your Word. Amen.

Hear my Prayer

Hear my cry, O God; listen to my prayer. Psalm 61:1

When you are driving, do you talk to yourself? Perhaps you keep a stream-of-consciousness monologue going: *OK, bank next, then carpool line, then.... Oh no, is today the 14th? Why do I always forget to get a card for John's mother? She never forgets my birthday...*

Or maybe you prefer one-sided conversations with other drivers. I often burst out with a muttered tirade: *Hey, buddy, quit tailgating! Give me some space! It's not my fault you're late to work!* Likely, it is just as well that others can't hear what we are saying.

Jesus told a parable about two men who went to the temple to pray. The first man, a Pharisee, supposedly was praying to God, but in reality was only boasting about himself: *God, I thank you that I am not like other people - robbers, evildoers, adulterers -or even like this tax collector.* (Luke 18:11) He may as well have been conversing with himself. The second man, the tax collector who had been scorned by the Pharisee, humbly pleaded to God for mercy: *God, have mercy on me, a sinner.* (Luke 18:13) Jesus made it clear that only the second man went home justified before God.

Prayer is to be a humble, two-way conversation with God. The Creator of the vast galaxies has deigned to hear us, so we should approach God with awe and reverence. But we are also encouraged to cry out to God as our loving Father who cares deeply for each of us as individuals.

Prayer for Today:

Dear Father and Creator, I come before you in humility, thankful that you truly care for me. I praise you for who You are and for all that you have done in my life. You already know my needs, but you have told us to bring our requests before you, so I do this now. Amen.

Fishtailing

Then we will no longer be infants, tossed back and forth by the waves, and blown here and there by every wind of teaching and by the cunning and craftiness of people in their deceitful scheming. Ephesians 4:14

Have you ever watched a video of a crash caused by trailer sway? It's a pretty terrifying sight. A slight bit of oscillation in the trailer causes the trailer to begin to fishtail. This escalates until the level of sway causes the trailer to flip over, swinging the tow vehicle around like a rag doll and endangering everyone in its vicinity.

The Bible warns us to avoid being blown back and forth by incorrect doctrines that are introduced by deceitful teachers. In Philippians, Paul uses the metaphor of an infant to describe anyone who sways off the course of accurate Biblical teaching. But why should I care about doctrine? Isn't that just the domain of scholars and preachers? Correct doctrine is critical for everyone because it sets forth exactly who God is and how we are to live in relation to Him. If we read blogs and listen to sermons that mishandle the Word of truth, we may absorb ideas about God that can leave us confused, frightened, or dangerously unaware of our need to repent. Paul instructed Timothy to provide careful instruction for the church: *"For the time will come when people will not put up with sound doctrine. Instead, to suit their own desires, they will gather around them a great number of teachers to say what their itching ears want to hear." (2 Timothy 4:3)*

There are preventative measures that can minimize trailer sway, such as proper weight distribution, installing an anti-sway device, and taking special care when going downhill or traveling on a windy day. Spiritual sway can be minimized by carefully testing what you read and hear to be sure that it aligns with the words of Scripture. Don't be an infant who only wants to hear enticing or easy ideas: learn and follow the truth.

Prayer for Today:

Dear God, I want to know you as you truly are.
I want to understand your Word correctly and
follow your teachings this day. Please grant
me discernment so that I will not wander away
from the truth. Amen.

Unfounded Worry

Therefore I tell you, do not worry about your life, what you will eat or drink; or about your body, what you will wear. Is not life more than food, and the body more than clothes? Look at the birds of the air; they do not sow or reap or store away in barns, and yet your heavenly Father feeds them.   Are you not much more valuable than they?   Can any one of you by worrying add a single hour to your life? Matthew 6:25-27

Near the town of Old Fort, North Carolina, Interstate 40 includes a curvy section with a steep six percent grade for approximately six miles. Several runaway truck ramps have been constructed on the downhill side for emergency use in case of brake failure. Even before purchasing our travel trailer, this stretch of road always made me extremely nervous. I would practically come to a standstill at the crest of the hill so that I could wait as long as possible before beginning to tap on the brake pedal. When we picked up our trailer in Tennessee, we planned a homeward route that would avoid the Old Fort grade. On our second camping trip, my husband presented three convincing reasons why it was now time to navigate Old Fort. 1. Our trailer brakes were sufficiently broken in. 2. He had gained enough towing experience. 3. We shouldn't be forced to travel on longer, alternate routes just because I was a worrier! As it turns out, the specialized tow package on our

Dodge Ram actually made the downhill journey less stressful than the journey had been in a car. Huge relief!

Jesus reminded his followers that worry could not add a single hour to their lives. Scientists tell us that worry can actually shorten our life due to the physiological effects of stress. So why do we continue to worry? Perhaps it is...
- the feeling that we are not in control of a situation
- the feeling that the situation is ours to control
- the problem is physically, mentally, or emotionally dangerous
- the problem is just plain annoying
- the situation is unfamiliar
- the situation is all too familiar

The antidote for worry, according to Jesus, is to notice God's faithfulness in feeding the birds. (Matthew 6:25-27) He also told his disciples to remember that He has overcome the world. (John 16:33) Paul's advice to believers was, "*Do not be anxious about anything, but in every situation, by prayer and petition, with thanksgiving, present your requests to God. And the peace of God, which transcends all understanding, will guard your hearts and your minds in Christ Jesus.* (Philippians 4:6-7)

Prayer for Today:

Dear God, you faithfully provide for the birds, and you can provide for me. The world is filled with trouble, but you have overcome the world. You already know my current situation, and you know the future. I present my requests to you now, and I ask that you grant me your wisdom and peace. Amen.

Managing Expectations

Yes, and I will continue to rejoice, for I know that through your prayers and God's provision of the Spirit of Jesus Christ what has happened to me will turn out for my deliverance. I eagerly expect and hope that I will in no way be ashamed, but will have sufficient courage so that now as always Christ will be exalted in my body, whether by life or by death. Philippians 1: 18-20

"I didn't expect to be wearing a jacket every day that we've been in Florida!" Somehow, my expectations for this trip had been a bit unrealistic, especially for the first week of January. In the same way, as Christians we often have the unrealistic idea that our lives will be free from sorrow, illness, or persecution. Jesus himself assured his followers, *I have told you these things, so that in me you may have peace. In this world you will have trouble. But take heart! I have overcome the world.* (John 16:33)

We should assume that our daily experience will mirror the common lot of others in terms of everyday problems and irritations. Beyond that, we should expect to encounter outright resistance because we identify ourselves as followers of Christ. This resistance might range from mild kidding to the loss of employment opportunities. The persecution may escalate to threats of physical harm or even to death. Jesus promises peace in all of these situations, a peace that is based on the assurance that He has overcome the world.

Paul wrote to the people of Philippi from a jail cell. He explained that his imprisonment had resulted in the truth of the gospel being proclaimed throughout the entire palace guard. In addition, Paul was aware that other believers had been strengthened and emboldened through his example. He confidently expected the provision of sufficient courage to continue serving and exalting Christ, whether by life or death. His confidence was based on the indwelling Spirit of Jesus and on his awareness that others were praying for him. (Philippians 1:18-20)

Let us not expect a type of life that Jesus never promised, but let us expect that Christ will grant to us strength and peace.

Prayer for Today:

Dear Lord, you know every situation that I will face today and in the future. You did not sugar coat the troubles of life or the cost of following you. Thank you for your promise of peace and for your assurance that you will never leave or forsake me. May I remember to pray for those around the world who are persecuted for your sake, and may I faithfully serve you today. Amen.

Who's My Boss?

Whatever you do, work at it with all your heart, as working for the Lord, not for human masters, since you know that you will receive an inheritance from the Lord as a reward. It is the Lord Christ you are serving. Colossians 3:23-24

My first part-time job was very mundane, working for minimum wage in a small store. The repetitive duties included tidying up the displays and re-stocking shelves under the harsh glare of florescent lights. The evening before I reported for work, my father gave me some wise advice. "Always remember," he said, "you aren't doing your employers a favor by working for them. They are doing you a favor by hiring you."

Over the years, working in positions as diverse as camp counselor, waitress, teacher, and moving company packer, I've had to remind myself (sometimes reluctantly) of my father's words during times of job - related stress. Many jobs just don't seem like a wonderful gift! Difficult co-workers, looming deadlines, and intense responsibilities can lead to complaints and less than stellar performance on the job. So how can I view my job in a positive light and persevere towards excellence?

Consider the words of Paul in Colossians 3:23: *Whatever you do, work at it with all your heart, as working for the Lord, not for human masters.* My employer has given me an opportunity, and God has asked me to regard my job as service done for the Lord. Am I bored? I can try to fulfill my duties more carefully. Am I harried and frustrated? I can remember that God is with me to guide and sustain. Is my attitude lousy? I can remind myself that the Lord is ultimately my boss and I answer to Him.

Prayer for Today:

Dear God, in everything that I do today, help me to work with excellence. May my attitudes and actions honor you. Amen.

God is Not Mocked

How long will the enemy mock you, God? Will the foe revile your name forever? Psalm 74:10

"We are going up to Jerusalem," he said, "and the Son of Man will be delivered over to the chief priests and the teachers of the law. They will condemn him to death and will hand him over to the Gentiles, who will mock him and spit on him, flog him and kill him. Three days later he will rise." Mark 10:33-34

Do not be deceived; God cannot be mocked. A man reaps what he sows. Galatians 6:7

Television shows and movies often provide depictions of RV travelers that are less than flattering. Some of the screenwriters create unlikeable characters who live in rusting campers and display obnoxious behavior. Recognizing that the shows are meant as satire might make it possible to ignore the fact that an activity we love is being derided, but the caricatures of popular culture can also be a bit embarrassing. We hope that our camping neighbors are thoughtful, intelligent, and clean, and if they are not, we don't want to be associated with them.

Throughout history, individuals and nations have chosen to openly mock God and His servants. The prophets were scorned and killed, Goliath shouted insults at David, and Pharaoh boldly stated, *who is the Lord, that I should obey him and let Israel go?* (Exodus 5:2) Christ was mocked and brutally crucified. Although we know that God always has the final word and in an ultimate sense can never be mocked, there are times when we don't enjoy being associated with God or His people. But this is exactly what we are called to do. The book of Acts describes Barnabas and Paul as *men who have risked their lives for the name of our Lord Jesus Christ.* (Acts 15:26) Jesus said, *Whoever wants to be my disciple must deny themselves and take up their cross daily and follow me.* (Luke 9:23) He also promised, *Be faithful, even to the point of death, and I will give you life as your victor's crown.* (Revelation 2:10)

Prayer for Today:

Dear Lord, many are mocking you and scorning your people this day. Help me never to be ashamed to identify with you. Thank you that the victory is yours. Amen.

Right of Way

See what great love the Father has lavished on us, that we should be called children of God! And that is what we are! 1 John 3:1

Yet to all who did receive him, to those who believed in his name, he gave the right to become children of God— John 1:12

RRRRrrrRRRrrrrRRrrr!" The siren of a fire truck is unmistakable. As soon as you hear its piercing sound, it is essential to yield the right of way. The driver of the fire truck even has the ability to change traffic signals along the route, not because of any innate power, but because the fire fighter acts in the authority of the fire department. The signals and the other drivers on the road recognize that authority and yield.

God sits enthroned in heaven, pure and almighty. The Bible says that He cannot look upon evil, and all of us have sinned. How can we ever earn the right to stand in his presence? We do not have the ability to stand there on the basis of our own moral efforts. But just as a little girl may enter the royal court of an emperor if the potentate is her father, we may come before God if we have been forgiven of our sins through belief in the sacrificial death of Christ on our behalf.

When we pray in the name of Jesus, we invoke the authority of our Savior. Jesus said, *Very truly I tell you, my*

Father will give you whatever you ask in my name. " (John 16:23) This does not mean that we can ask to win the lottery! We must ask in accordance with the character and will of Christ. As we study the Scriptures, our petitions will become more and more closely aligned with what is appropriate for a child of God.

Prayer for Today:

Dear Lord, thank you that you have made a way for me to become your child. Thank you for forgiving my sins through the sacrificial death of your Son. May I pray in your name for those things that honor you. Your power and authority can open doors and defeat evil. Amen.

My Soul Sings

Sing joyfully to the Lord, you righteous; it is fitting for the upright to praise him. Psalm 33:1

Hymn writers through the ages have penned lyrics and melodies which praise God for the awesome wonders of creation. Even agnostics and atheists can feel tranquility and joy in the presence of nature's marvels. Why do our souls sing when we view a gorgeous wilderness panorama? The beauty and complexity of the natural world is a visible manifestation of the power and creativity of God. Beyond that, our response to nature also reveals that God has made us with souls and spirits. We are not amoebas or automatons, but creatures made in the image of God. What else does the Bible teach us through creation?

We should admire creation and seek to preserve its beauty, but we should never revere it above God. In Romans 1:25, Paul denounces those who ex*changed the truth about God for a lie, and worshiped and served created things rather than the Creator.*

Creation creates accountability before God. *For since the creation of the world God's invisible qualities-his eternal power and divine nature-have been clearly seen, being understood from what has been made, so that people are without excuse.* (Romans 1:20)

A God who is powerful and wise enough to create the universe does not grow weary or lack understanding. *The Lord is the everlasting God, the Creator of the ends of the earth. He will not grow tired or weary, and his understanding no one can fathom.* (Isaiah 40:28)

Prayer for Today:

Dear Father, my heart soars when I view the grandeur and intricacy of the universe, and so I sing to you from my soul today. May my thoughts always turn to you as I travel in the world that you have created. Amen.

Bigger Barns

And he told them this parable. "The ground of a certain rich man yielded an abundant harvest. He thought to himself, "What shall I do? I have no place to store my crops." Then he said, "This is what I'll do. I will tear down my barns and build bigger ones, and there I will store my surplus grain. And I'll say to myself, 'You have plenty of grain laid up for many years. Take life easy; eat, drink and be merry.'" But God said to him, "You fool! This very night your life will be demanded from you. Then who will get what you have prepared for yourself?" This is how it will be with whoever stores up things for themselves but is not rich toward God. Luke 12:16-21*

One day, Jesus was teaching his disciples when a man blurted out a request for Christ to arbitrate an inheritance dispute for him. Jesus refused to get involved in the man's legal conflict. He recognized that the man was filled with greed, so he spoke the parable of the rich fool. The fool had a large crop surplus, so he planned to tear down his barns, build bigger barns, and live out his days in leisure. He was not a fool for being rich; he was a fool because his overwhelming focus was on selfishly enjoying his wealth without realizing that his days were numbered.

Immediately upon finishing the parable, Jesus reminded his listeners that while the birds have no storage barns, God feeds them. We can rely on God's provision as we seek His kingdom above all else. God clothes the lilies of the field, and He knows our needs. We are to give generously to others, trusting in the faithfulness of God.

Do you have a storage barn for your RV? Perhaps you were forced to build or rent one because housing covenants in your neighborhood prohibit the storage of anything other than family vehicles on your property. Perhaps you chose a specialized enclosure in order to better protect your rig. In either situation, having a storage building, even a fancy one, is not a sin. The sin would be a preoccupation with the things that we own. Jesus preceded his parable with the statement, *life does not consist in an abundance of possessions.* (Luke 12:15) If our thoughts, plans, and happiness are too closely linked to our belongings, then we are teetering on the edge of greed.

The antidote for greed is generosity, and the source of cheerful generosity is being *rich toward God.* (Luke 12:21) Generosity also increases when we consciously decide to trust in God as the ultimate provider for all of our needs.

Prayer for Today:

Thank you, Lord, that you provide for the ravens and for me. May I never be reluctant to show generosity toward others because I lack trust in you. I am thankful for the many blessings that you have given to me. Please show me specific ways that I can pass on your blessings to others. Amen.

Peer Pressure

Do not conform to the pattern of this world, but be transformed by the renewing of your mind. Then you will be able to test and approve what God's will is - his good, pleasing and perfect will. Romans 12:2

Peer pressure isn't just for teenagers. We've all had the experience of traveling down a two-lane road with a line of cars forming behind us, the other drivers trying to bully us into going faster. At that moment, we may actually be speeding ourselves, perhaps by three or four miles per hour, but this doesn't satisfy the lead-footed motorists to the rear. So we are left with only two options. We can either stubbornly continue at our current speed and risk getting rear-ended, or we can gradually increase our pace and risk being pulled over by the police.

There are many moral issues in life for which our choices mirror the speed limit options. We may feel pressured to view movies and television shows that dishonor God in order to carry on conversations at the workplace. We may experience coercion to gossip or falsify accounting documents. Each time that we move outside our comfort zone, we hope to have satisfied others, but in reality they are rarely placated. Although we should not pompously present ourselves in a holier-than-thou manner, it's important that we maintain a lifestyle that glorifies God.

91

Romans 12:2 provides a solution to the problem of conformity to our surrounding culture. We are to be transformed through the renewing of our minds. This can occur over time as we fill our minds with the truths of Scripture and meditate on what is good, pure, and right. In this way, our minds will more and more often default to honorable and uplifting attitudes, thoughts, and perspectives. When our minds are transformed, eventually our actions will also be transformed for our good and God's glory.

Prayer for Today:

Dear God, there are so many times when I feel pressured to give in little by little to sinful actions or thoughts. Please transform me by the renewing of my mind. May I be a gracious, gentle example of the joy of walking in your truth.

Added Value?

I am sending you out like sheep among wolves. Therefore be as shrewd as snakes and as innocent as doves. Be on your guard; you will be handed over to the local councils and be flogged in the synagogues. On my account you will be brought before governors and kings as witnesses to them and to the Gentiles. But when they arrest you, do not worry about what to say or how to say it. At that time you will be given what to say, for it will not be you speaking, but the Spirit of your Father speaking through you. Matthew 10:16-20

Have you noticed that some businesses provide "freebies" in an attempt to make the customer perceive that their product or service has added value? The free items could range from inexpensive candy in a dish at the checkout counter, to a cold bottle of water as you wait for an appointment, to several years of free oil changes for those who buy a vehicle. In each case, you might be more likely to make a purchase or to have a positive feeling about the business as a result of receiving a gift.

This business strategy can backfire if the customer feels that the free items are unnecessary, or if the buyer realizes that the "added value" is actually added into the price. Free shipping isn't really free, and that complimentary bag of popcorn in the hardware store has an unannounced cost as well.

Careful shopping can help us avoid purchasing pitfalls, but Jesus warned his disciples to be "shrewd as snakes" for a more important reason than saving money. His followers would soon be encountering severe persecution because of their message. Their lives were to be completely innocent, like doves, but they were also to be marked by alert shrewdness and reliance on the Holy Spirit. They were to be on their guard, yet dependent on the Spirit for their spoken defense.

Prayer for Today:

Dear God, we have been told to expect persecution and to be on our guard. May my moral character have such purity that I am blameless before You and others. When opposition arises, may my actions be clear-sighted, and may I calmly be guided by your Spirit. Amen

Low Bridge Ahead

The prudent see danger and take refuge, but the simple keep going and pay the penalty. Proverbs 27:12

Some type of warning is needed in order to avoid disaster at a low bridge clearance. Perhaps you have viewed online videos that show the tops of campers or trucks being peeled back like the lid of a sardine can. Either the drivers in the videos ignored the warning signs, or they didn't have an accurate measurement of their rig's height, or they simply had traveled past the last opportunity to turn around and take another route.

Warning systems for travel can include signs, lights, and phone apps. Spiritual warning systems available to us are the words of Scripture, the advice of wise individuals, and our inner sense that something isn't quite right. None of those systems will work if they are ignored.

It's easy to want to continue down a path that is not pleasing to God because we are too embarrassed to admit our mistake. We also tend to keep going on an ill-advised path when we have invested a great deal of time, money, or emotional energy on that road. Unfortunately, if we don't change course, we may reach a point in which a catastrophe is inevitable. God desires to protect us from such a calamity.

Prayer for Today:

Dear Lord, your Word has been provided as a light for my path, and I need to study it in order to be forewarned about dangers ahead. I also need to listen to the wisdom of godly individuals and to the inner "red flags" that you send. Please help me to make wise decisions today that will lead me away from unhelpful or unsafe situations. May I not deceive myself by thinking that I am above giving in to temptation. May I not consider myself as too smart to become entrapped in a perilous situation. I know that I need to listen carefully to your voice today. Thank you for your great love for me. Amen.

The Winds Obey Him

Suddenly a furious storm came up on the lake, so that the waves swept over the boat. The disciples went and woke him, saying, "Lord, save us! We're going to drown! He replied, "You of little faith, why are you so afraid?" Then he got up and rebuked the winds and the waves, and it was completely calm. The men were amazed and asked, "What kind of man is this? Even the winds and the waves obey him!"
Matthew 8:24-27

A puff...a breeze...a gust...suddenly the wind sensor on the awning of your camper gets the message and the awning begins to retract. Any glitch in this process could lead to the destruction of the awning and an expensive repair. Wind and storms are powerful forces of nature that should not be ignored.

The Bible records a scene in which Jesus and the disciples are in a boat, crossing a large lake. At some point on the journey, Jesus has fallen asleep. A fierce squall comes up, but the disciples do not immediately wake the Lord. Perhaps they are reluctant to bother him after a long day of ministry. Or maybe they are too absorbed in trying to maintain control of the boat. Matthew tells us that the storm is furious and the waters are raging over the edge of the boat when the disciples finally seek the Lord's help.

After awakening Jesus, they call out frantically, *Teacher, don't you care if we drown?* (Mark 4:38) Jesus verbally rebukes the wind and waves, and immediately the storm ceases and the surface of the water becomes smooth. This astounding demonstration of the Lord's power over creation causes the disciples to tremble in terror. They now grasp more fully that Jesus is not merely another teacher or prophet.

Like the disciples, we sometimes are reluctant to ask for the help of Christ. Maybe we feel that our need is too insignificant to bother him, or perhaps we doubt his ability to help. We try to work out the situation in our own wisdom and strength. Our problem turns from a puff of wind to a dangerous gale before we seek his assistance. Jesus is already aware of our situation, but he desires that we bring our requests and our worries to him. *Cast all your anxiety on him because he cares for you.* (1 Peter 5:7)

Prayer for Today:

Dear Lord, you had compassion on the
disciples and met them in their time of need,
demonstrating your awesome power and love.
I humbly bring my concerns and needs before
you today. Please increase my faith and guide
me with your wisdom. Amen.

Local Flavor

Then your Father, who sees what is done in secret, will reward you.
Matthew 6:4

When we aren't trying to cover too many miles in a day, it's fun to try out "hole in the wall" restaurants in small towns. We recently parked on a tiny main street, hoping to eat at a highly-rated fish restaurant, only to discover that the place was closed on Mondays. So we strolled across the street, where we found a wonderful taqueria with delicious food. It was great to help keep this little place in business, and our meal was a refreshing change from chain restaurants and rest area picnics.

Small town restaurant owners work hard, often in obscurity, until word gets around about the quality of the food and service. Long hours can lead to only small returns as they struggle to establish a business. Perhaps you feel that no one takes notice of your actions as you toil at your job, lovingly raise your children, or serve as a volunteer. Jesus sees you. The Bible reminds us to do our work as unto the Lord, putting forth excellence in effort and cultivating purity in our motives and attitudes. The difficulty of our situation may not change, but Christ is with us to guide and to help.

Prayer for Today:

Dear God, you are the Lord of all. You always know my actions and my inner thoughts. You have promised to never leave or forsake me. May all that I do today be done with a positive attitude and with honorable effort. Amen.

Should I Be Transparent?

You have searched me, Lord, and you know me. You know when I sit and when I rise; you perceive my thoughts from afar...Search me, God, and know my heart; test me and know my anxious thoughts. See if there is any offensive way in me, and lead me in the way everlasting.
Psalm 139:1-2, 23-24

Many campers are designed with dual window shades for day and evening use. The daytime shades are partially concealing, and the evening shades are almost opaque. Of course, if neither shade is used, the transparent window will allow anyone outdoors to easily view the inside of your rig. I love having the light stream through the windows as much as possible, so I have to remind myself to maintain the proper amount of privacy by adjusting the shades.

Should we be emotionally transparent before others? Although honesty and openness are commendable, it's not advisable to be totally transparent with everyone that we meet. Not all those that we encounter need to know of our trials, inner turmoil, and regrets. But we also should not put up a facade of false cheer or holier-than-thou religiosity that turns away others.

Is it possible to be anything but transparent before God? In an ultimate sense, no. God created us, and he knows every cell in our body and every thought that we consider. Nothing can be hidden from God. Yet the psalmist specifically asked God to search him for anything offensive that might lie within. He also asked the Lord to lead him in the way everlasting. The light of God's truth is illuminating and brings us more into conformity with His character. Let us never shrink from the inspection of the Almighty.

Prayer for Today:

Dear Heavenly Father, nothing is hidden from your sight. You created me, and you know everything about me, even the words that I will say before I speak them. May I be open to the searching of my heart. Whatever you see that is offensive to you, please reveal it to me, and may I respond in obedience to this revelation. Amen.

Need S'more Patience?

But if we hope for what we do not yet have, we wait for it patiently.
Romans 8:25

My mother was a Junior Girl Scout leader, and even before I was old enough to join my sister's troop, I was allowed to tag along on weekend camping trips. At campfire time, the Scouts were excited about creating S'mores from graham crackers, chocolate bars, and marshmallows. I detested marshmallows, but I adored working with fire: sparking tinder, adding twigs, and stirring the coals were all very satisfying. Before long, the older girls in the troop enlisted me as their "mascot" and chief marshmallow cooker. Because I didn't want to eat the fluffy treats, I had the patience to gently cook them to golden brown perfection. The girls who wanted to eat their marshmallows right away often held them too close to the fire and ended up with scorched, flaming torches rather than edible marshmallows.

The Scriptures often link patience with hope. The concept of hope in the Bible is that of confident expectation. It is not mere wishful thinking. Because God is faithful, our hope is not misplaced. As an experienced marshmallow roaster, I was confident that if I would patiently check the fire, twirl the marshmallow slowly, and keep away from the hottest coals, I would end up with a finished product that the older Scouts would love. In the same way, reminding myself of the consistency and power of God is helpful during difficult times when I find it very hard to be patient. Ralph Waldo Emerson said, "All I have seen teaches me to trust the creator for all I have not seen." I have seen God working in my life and in the lives of others; therefore, I will seek to patiently wait on his timing.

Prayer for Today:

O gracious and faithful Heavenly Father, you are utterly consistent in your character and loving in your dealings with me. I know that you have the power to bring your promises to fruition. Grant me the ability to patiently wait on you. Amen.

First Impressions

Suppose a man comes into your meeting wearing a gold ring and fine clothes, and a poor man in filthy old clothes also comes in. If you show special attention to the man wearing fine clothes and say, "Here's a good seat for you," but say to the poor man, "You stand there" or "Sit on the floor by my feet," have you not discriminated among yourselves and become judges with evil thoughts? James 2:2-4

When hiking down a trail, have you ever suddenly become aware that you are forming instant opinions regarding everyone that you encounter hiking in the other direction? Maybe your thought process goes something like this: *Wow, he's tall...that mom needs to control her kids...if he would just trim that beard he would look a whole lot better...flip flops are not the smartest choice for a trail hike...*

It's natural to notice the physical attributes of others, but unfortunately I am often guilty of moving past noticing into judging. I've never met these individuals and don't know their backstories, and yet I have formed split-second opinions about their lives. In the second chapter of James, judging is linked both to evil thoughts and to making distinctions among people. An example is given in which a rich stranger and a poor stranger enter a Christian meeting. If the rich man is given preferential attention based on his wealthy appearance, those who have discriminated in this way are called out as being evil.

In church meetings or on the trail, it's all too easy to size someone up instantly. It may well be the case that the shabbily dressed individual who enters our assembly will turn out to be a loving, helpful, or spiritually mature person. If we snub the people who don't pass our initial visual inspection, they may never return, and our group will be all the poorer spiritually. As I travel far from home, I can make a conscious effort to avoid mental judgements. If someone stands out physically, I can seek to just take notice but not turn that into an opinion. If someone comes across as annoying, I can recognize that I don't know all the details of that person's life. If someone is displaying a blatant disregard for God, I can pray for them.

The final section of James 2 provides a solution to judgmental distinctions: *Speak and act as those who are going to be judged by the law that gives freedom, because judgment without mercy will be shown to anyone who has not been merciful. Mercy triumphs over judgment.* (James 2:12-13)

Prayer for Today:

Dear God, please forgive me when I judge others based on a fleeting encounter. Help me to compassionately pray for those who make a negative impression on me, and help me to be full of grace and mercy towards others. Amen.

Bear Aware

For the Lord gives wisdom; from his mouth come knowledge and understanding. He holds success in store for the upright, he is a shield to those whose walk is blameless, for he guards the course of the just and protects the way of his faithful ones. Proverbs 2:6-8

Alexander Springs Campground in the Ocala National Forest lies in the heart of alligator country, but the overwhelming message that is communicated to campers is "Be Bear Aware!" In order to discourage bears from wandering into campsites to forage for food, each site is equipped with bear-resistant storage boxes. Forest Service literature explains how to avoid or escape from bear encounters on the trail. Anyone encountering a bear is advised to stand tall with arms extended. This can sometimes trick the bear into believing that you are much larger than your actual size. Bears actually have decent eyesight – at least as good as that of humans, and their night vision is especially strong. So it's wise to avoid encountering a bear in the first place.

There are many situations in life for which "avoiding the bear" is preferable to "escaping the bear". Keeping alert to our physical surroundings will make us less likely to become trapped in a difficult or dangerous setting. Whether on a trail or in a parking lot, it's wise to stay vigilant.

Challenging or distressing emotional circumstances can sometimes be eluded as well. Listening to our inner warning voice can help us to steer clear of destructive relationships. If we refrain from hasty involvement in situations that have little chance of a positive outcome, we can save ourselves much misery.

There are also spiritual pitfalls that are best avoided. Pulling isolated Bible verses out of context can lead to errors in interpretation. Following individual religious leaders more fervently than we follow Christ can leave us feeling disillusioned when those leaders do not live up to our expectations. Trying to serve God without the encouragement and support of other believers can become discouraging. We can dodge many spiritual hazards by consistently reading God's word and staying in fellowship with those who can provide help, discernment, and grace.

Prayer for Today:

Dear Heavenly Father, may your Scriptures
guide my ways. Please grant me foresight and
insight in my life that will help me avoid
physical, spiritual, and emotional dangers.
Amen.

Put on Your Boots

How long will you lie there, you sluggard? When will you get up from your sleep? A little sleep, a little slumber, a little folding of the hands to rest-and poverty will come on you like a thief and scarcity like an armed man. Proverbs 6:9-11

An experienced drill instructor once told his platoon, "Many battles have been lost because some guy didn't want to put on his boots." I often thought of this quote in my backpacking days. On cold mornings, it was so hard to get out of a warm sleeping bag, put on half-frozen boots, open the zipper on the tent, and stagger out to make breakfast. Now that I camp in a travel trailer, the morning routine is much less daunting. Yet it is still easy to resist getting started on necessary tasks, both on the road and at home. The result will probably not be the loss of a physical battle, but there could be mental battles lost or time wasted.

For example, if I have been struggling to establish an exercise routine, each time I delay getting dressed in my jogging clothes I am more likely to get distracted by other pursuits. I may never get around to exercising at all on that particular day. In a similar fashion, if I notice a book that has been left on the counter, think about putting it away, and put off that little chore for another time, I am left with a cluttered counter and a growing To Do list.

My mantra for the beginning of this calendar year was "Do it Now." I'm making a conscious effort to complete little tasks as soon as I think of them, whenever possible. I'm not sure how much time I've saved, but I know that I feel very satisfied to have accomplished so many small errands. It's a relief to not have to revisit thoughts about a single job over and over.

Prayer for Today:

Dear Lord, may I be diligent when it is constructive, and may I be flexible when you have unexpected plans for me today. Help me to be conscientious but not overly rigid as I approach the tasks that could be accomplished. Amen.

Not a Chance Encounter

Now an angel of the Lord said to Philip, "Go south to the road - the desert road -that leads from Jerusalem to Gaza." So he started out, and on his way he met an Ethiopian eunuch...Then Philip ran up to the chariot and heard the man reading Isaiah the prophet...Then Philip began with that very passage of Scripture and told him the good news about Jesus. Acts 8:26-27, 30, 35

"This can't be correct!" We were traveling in Tennessee, heading to an outdoor festival. The two lane road had narrowed and turned to gravel, dusk was fast approaching, and we were getting low on gas. Some rather sketchy looking properties dotted the landscape, and I began to be concerned for our safety. Suddenly a small sign appeared on our right: *Now Entering North Carolina.* What? Somehow we had veered off course far enough to have circled back into our home state.

The road soon came to an abrupt end, and there we discovered a young woman standing next to her car with a road map spread across the hood. Like us, she was lost and a bit nervous, and as we spoke with her we began to realize that our encounter with this woman was not coincidental. She had just studied the pathway out and could lead the way. She also could help if our car should run out of fuel before arriving at the nearest gas station. Our family was able to assist her by

111

ensuring that she would not have to travel the dark road alone.
Thank you, God!

The Lord of space and time was looking out for the needs
of our family and of this stranger well before the moment when
our paths intersected. In a similar way, the Book of Acts tells
how Philip met an Ethiopian eunuch on a remote desert road.
The eunuch was sitting in his chariot, reading the very portion
of the Book of Isaiah which foretells the suffering of Christ.
He was seeking exactly what Philip could provide: an
explanation of this section of Scripture. Philip's divine
encounter with this man gave him a perfect opportunity to
explain how Jesus fulfilled prophetic revelation. Philip was
able to help the Ethiopian find true faith in Jesus as the
Messiah.

Prayer for Today:

Dear God, you know my future and what my
needs will be. Thank you for promising to
work all things together for my good. When
you provide divine encounters with those who
are seeking You, may I notice them and be
faithful to tell of your goodness and mercy.
Amen.

The Secret Things Belong to the Lord

The secret things belong to the Lord our God, but the things revealed belong to us and to our children forever, that we may follow all the words of this law. Deuteronomy 29:29

When on the road, we try to glean as much information as possible about potential campgrounds via online resources and word-of-mouth recommendations from those we trust. I especially appreciate websites that show photographs of every campsite in a particular park. But there are times when we have to make a decision with minimal information, leaving us a bit uneasy until we actually arrive and (hopefully) breathe a sigh of relief.

On our faith journey, it is normal to have sincere questions and some lingering doubts that can cause us to feel unsettled. God's ways are higher than the ways of mankind, and He has chosen not to explain everything about Himself. But this is not a valid reason to excuse ourselves from following the parts of His Word that we do comprehend.

The Bible promises in Deuteronomy 29:29 that enough about God has been revealed to enable us to follow His law successfully. We will never have all of our difficult theological questions answered, for *the secret things belong to the Lord.* But many truths have been revealed to us through the Scriptures that we can understand. God has also revealed His awesome power, order, and creativity through the wonders of creation. He has revealed His faithfulness through the experiences of believers who have gone before us or who accompany us on our journey today. If we sincerely desire to follow His commands, everything that we need to be successful has been provided for us and for our children forever.

Prayer for Today:

Dear God, your ways are unsearchable, and we will never completely understand them. Thank you that you have revealed so many things about Yourself. Thank you that what you have chosen to reveal is sufficient for me to follow You. May future generations honor You because I make a decision today to trust and obey you through faith. Amen.

Roadside Attractions

He had no beauty or majesty to attract us to him, nothing in his appearance that we should desire him. Isaiah 53:2

Sometimes it's fun to get off the interstate highways and travel down less crowded paths. On these roads, you are likely to encounter some interesting roadside attractions (not to mention delicious food at local diners.) Some of the more quirky stops are the World's Largest Ball of Twine in Cawker City, Kansas, and Carhenge in Alliance, Nebraska. The small towns near these curiosities benefit from the patronage of extra visitors each year who end up buying gas or supplies.

Beautiful women are said to be attractive, magnets attract metal, and roadside attractions draw in gawkers. In what way did Jesus attract people? In Isaiah chapter 53, the prophet makes it clear that the coming Messiah would not be physically attractive. *He had no beauty or majesty to attract us to him, nothing in his appearance that we should desire him.* (Isaiah 53:2) Crowds were attracted to his wisdom and miracles. *Where did this man get these things?" they asked. "What's this wisdom that has been given him? What are these remarkable miracles he is performing?"* (Mark 6:2)

Our culture places such a high value on physical beauty that even infants who are especially lovely receive a great deal of positive attention.   Yet when those same children become teenagers or young adults, they may begin to wonder if those who profess a romantic interest in them truly understand and love them for more than just their outward appearance.

How should we approach physical attractiveness? Whether or not we are outwardly handsome or beautiful, we should seek to develop a gracious personality and upright character,   Peter, speaking specifically to women, counseled them to cultivate *the unfading beauty of a gentle and quiet spirit, which is of great worth in God's sight.* (1 Peter 3:4) When we look at others, we can resist our natural inclination to immediately judge on outward appearances. The children in our sphere of influence will benefit greatly from being complimented on their admirable inner qualities. Finally, whenever we are tempted to fixate on our own appearance, we can train our mind to focus elsewhere. W*hatever is true, whatever is noble, whatever is right, whatever is pure, whatever is lovely, whatever is admirable - if anything is excellent or praiseworthy - think about such things.* (Philippians 4:8)

Prayer for Today:
Dear God, I thank you that when you sent your
Son into this world, it was not his outward
appearance that attracted others. May I never
give undue importance to external beauty.
Please create in me a character and a
personality that honor you. Amen.

116

Stressful Relaxation?

Yes, my soul, find rest in God; my hope comes from him. Psalm 62:5

Why is preparing to relax sometimes so stressful? We visualize ourselves spending a lovely weekend along a burbling stream. Then we begin to plan, purchase, load up, drive off, sit in traffic, drive on, back in, set up, and on and on it goes. We may start to feel frazzled and more in need of a vacation than we were at the outset! Yet we can still achieve some degree of relaxation if we will take a deep breath and find joy in the journey.

The truest type of rest is rest of the soul, and that is only available with God's help. Soul rest is deep and abiding, even when earthly situations are frantic or troubling and when our emotions will not cooperate. The spiritual equivalent of taking a deep breath is to be still and ask God for calmness of soul. The spiritual equivalent of finding joy in the journey is to remind ourselves that Christ promised to never leave or forsake us. We are never alone, and the Lord is in control. Trust that he can grant an underlying inner serenity on every road of life.

It is also helpful to remember our hope and our destination: eternal life with God and with the saints who have gone before us. The apostle Paul experienced many trials: persecution, flogging, shipwreck, and illness. Yet when he referred to these trials in his second letter to the Corinthians, he stated, *For our light and momentary troubles are achieving for us an eternal glory that far outweighs them all. So we fix our eyes not on what is seen, but on what is unseen, since what is seen is temporary, but what is unseen is eternal.* (2 Corinthians 4:17-18)

Prayer for Today:

Dear Heavenly Father, thank you that we are designed for communion with you. May I remember that my soul can rest in you even when my circumstances bring discouragement and worry. Help me to be still and know that you are God. Amen.

Freely Give Grace

Freely you have received; freely give.   Matthew 10:8

"What goes around, comes around." This phrase is often quoted to express belief in karma, the idea that a person's good or bad deeds affect their future in this life, and possibly in future lives. While the Bible does teach the idea of cause and effect, it rejects the idea that human beings can earn eternal favor with God. Instead, we rely on the grace of God, the unmerited favor poured out on us because Christ paid the penalty for our sins.

Once we have received God's grace, the natural response should be to generously give grace to others. What might that look like as travelers and campers? How can we demonstrate grace in our actions, thoughts, and attitudes while on the road?

- Taking a deep breath and waiting patiently when the family ahead of you on the campground road is having a tough time backing into their site.
- Offering advice or a helping hand IF someone is open to that.
- Praying for those we encounter who are sullen, rude, or selfish.
- Giving our traveling companion encouragement and a listening ear.

- Allowing someone to step ahead of us in line.
- Disciplining our inner thoughts to avoid immediately judging others.
- Reminding ourselves that the grace of God has enabled us to receive forgiveness.

Prayer for Today:

Dear Heavenly Father, you have showered grace and forgiveness upon me through your son Jesus Christ. May my thoughts, words, and actions be filled with grace toward others. Help me to be creative in looking for ways to show grace today. Amen.

About the Author

Nancy Bell Kimsey is a lifelong outdoor enthusiast whose hiking and camping experiences have ranged from backpacking and family tent camping to adventuring in a fiberglass travel trailer. She moved to North Carolina to attend Wake Forest University and remained in the Tar Heel State throughout her career as an educator. When she's not writing or camping, Nancy enjoys sewing upcycled creations and singing with her church worship team and a local community chorale. Her writing has been published in *Women Who Served*, *The Secret Place*, and *Christian Women's Voice*.

CPSIA information can be obtained
at www.ICGtesting.com
Printed in the USA
BVHW031001021221
623082BV00015B/355

9 781736 773116